Bathrooms
Remodeling Projects

Bathrooms
Remodeling Projects

David H. Jacobs, Jr.

TAB Books

Division of McGraw-Hill, Inc.

New York San Francisco Washington, D.C. Auckland Bogotá
Caracas Lisbon London Madrid Mexico City Milan
Montreal New Delhi San Juan Singapore
Sydney Tokyo Toronto

© 1995 by **TAB Books**
Published by TAB Books, a division of McGraw-Hill, Inc.

pbk   2 3 4 5 6 7 8 9 DOC/DOC 9 9 8 7 6 5

Library of Congress Cataloging-in-Publication Data

Jacobs, David H.
    Bathrooms : remodeling projects / by David H. Jacobs, Jr.
       p.   cm.
    Includes index.
    ISBN 0-07-032405-0 (pbk.)
    1. Bathrooms—Remodeling—Amateurs' manuals. I. Title.
 TH4816.3.B37J33 1994
    643'.52—dc20   94-30231
                                                              CIP

Acquisitions editor: April Nolan
Editorial team: Joanne Slike, Executive Editor
              Joann Woy, Indexer
Production team: Katherine G. Brown, Director
              Ollie Harmon, Coding
              Jan Fisher, Desktop Operator   0324050
Designer: Jaclyn J. Boone   HT1

Acknowledgments

I have been most fortunate to receive a great deal of support and assistance while remodeling bathrooms, taking hundreds of pictures, writing, and putting together this book. For all of their encouragement, interest, and accommodations, I must thank the following people:

Jack Hori, senior vice president, and Roy Thompson, product marketing manager, for Makita U.S.A., Inc., were instrumental in numerous ways. I am most thankful for their support and the superior service I continue to receive from their Makita power tools and equipment.

My appreciation is extended to Francis Hummel, director of marketing for The Stanley Works, for his valuable contributions. It is a pleasure working with Stanley's quality hand tools, hardware, and other implements of all kinds.

Peter Fetterer, manager of media and civic services for Kohler Company, provided a tremendous amount of support for this book. Kohler Company offers a huge assortment of beautiful and fine crafted bathroom fixtures and accessories. All of the installation instructions provided with Kohler's products are precise and simple to comprehend. Customer service is second to none.

I want to thank David Martel, marketing manager for Central Purchasing, Inc., (Harbor Freight Tools), for his interest and support. Many tools and pieces of equipment from Harbor Freight Tools helped make small work of large projects.

Tom Tracy, advertising manager for Eagle Windows and Doors, has been most supportive. I thank him for his genuine interest and assistance. Likewise, I appreciate the excellent customer service I received from John Stearns, general manager of the Bellevue, Washington, Eagle Window and Door Center.

I appreciate the continued support provided by Thomas Marsh, vice president of marketing, and Daryl Hower, business manager, for Leslie-Locke, Inc. Their knowledge of roof windows, skylights, ventilation accessories, and other household products is first class.

Campbell Hausfeld air compressors and pneumatic equipment have been enormously helpful. For all of her assistance, I thank Hilarie Meyer, Campbell Hausfeld's associate merchandising manager.

In addition, I would like to express my most sincere appreciation to the following people and the companies or organizations they represent:

Maryann Olson, project coordinator/public relations for the American Plywood Association; Betty Talley, manager of marketing services, and Jeff Barnes for American Tool Companies, Inc.; Tina Alexiess, product manager for Autodesk Retail Products; Patricia McGirr, marketing manager for Alta Industries; Victor Lopez, technical services manager for Behr Process Corporation; Don Meucci, marketing director for the Cedar Shake and Shingle Bureau; Kim Garretson and Rich Sharp for DAP, Inc.; Jim Roadcap for The Eastwood Company; Matt Ragland, marketing manager for Empire Brushes, Inc.; Jim Brewer, marketing manager for Freud; Mike Cunningham, director of corporate communications for General Cable Company (Romex); Philip Martin, product marketing manager for Häfele America Company; Karin Martin, marketing services supervisor, and Jeff Bucar, marketing manager for Halo Lighting (Cooper Lighting); Dave Shanahan, director of marketing for Keller Industries, Inc.; Mario Mattich, director of Public Relations for Leviton Manufacturing Company, Inc.; Peter Wallace, senior vice president for McGuire Nicholas Company, Inc.; Ruth Tudor, product publicity manager for NuTone; Jim Schmiedeskamp and Phyllis Camesano for Owens-Corning Fiberglas Insulation; Mr. Dana Young, vice president of marketing for PanelLift Telpro, Inc.; Greg Hook, communications manager for PlumbShop; Bill Cork, public relations manager for Plano Molding Company; Bob McCully, vice president of sales and marketing for Power Products Company (SIMKAR); Robert Suarez, sales manager for Quality Doors; Rob Guzikowski, marketing manager for Simpson Strong-Tie Connector Company, Inc.; Jim Richeson, president of

Sta-Put Color Pegs; Dick Warden, general manager for Structron Corporation; Marty Sennett for DuPont Tyvek; Matthew Smith, marketing manager for U.S. Ceramic Tile Company; Beth Wintermantel, marketing communications manager for Weiser Lock; Timm Locke, product and publicity manager for the Western Wood Products Association; and Sue Gomez, marketing customer service manager for Zircon Corporation.

Brian Lord, Bob Greer, Jim Yocum, John Gittings, Steve Hayes, Ken Whitehair, and Josh Pearson provided lots of hands-on assistance, along with an ever entertaining array of antics and words of encouragement. Van and Kim Nordquist worked overtime to turn hundreds of film negatives into quality prints. Scott Wakeford and Al Davis, building inspectors for the City of Mercer Island, were most patient and helpful. For all of their efforts, I am most grateful.

As always, my family deserves credit for helping out whenever and wherever they could. I thank my wife, Janna, for all of her support and prompt attention to so many different details. I also appreciate the help offered by our children, their spouses and friends; Nicholas, Luke, Bethany, Ashleigh, Matthew, Adam, Brittany, Courtney, Kirsten, Terri, Steve, Whitney, Tyler, Shannon, Joey, Ryan Stearns, Steve Emanuels, and Daniel Dodson.

Finally, I want to thank Kim Tabor, editor-in-chief; April Nolan, acquisitions editor; and the entire editorial staff of TAB Books for their encouragement and support.

David H. Jacobs, Jr.

CONTENTS

Bᴀᴛʜʀᴏᴏᴍs are remodeled for many different reasons. Old age and years of use take their toll on once brilliant shines reflected by newer fixtures and accessories. Water seepage into cracked tile grout and hardened caulking cause dry rot and other significant structural damage. Lifestyles change and with them new bathroom appearances become prevalent concerns.

Homeowners by the thousands hire professional contractors, plumbers, electricians, and other tradespeople to completely remodel their bathrooms at costs that generally range from $5,000 to $9,000. Of course, those figures could go higher, depending on bathroom size, type of accessory installations, and sheer elegance desired.

Larger families, complete home updates, and changes in overall home atmospheres also figure into why homeowners prefer to remodel bathrooms. The question is, how in-depth does a bathroom remodel have to be to satisfy your wishes?

As long as major bathroom fixtures and their surrounding structures are in good condition, with no water leakage or dry rot problems, your bathroom might be well served with a new coat of paint, some wallpaper, a couple of pictures, and a plant or two. If sinks are chipped, faucets corroded, tile cracked, and bathtub finishes dulled beyond repair, it might be time to strip your bathroom down to the walls and install new fixtures, along with a new floor covering, some paint, wallpaper, plants, and so on.

If water seepage has caused paint to peel, caulking, grout, and tiles to fall away from walls, and resulted in stains on the floor, prepare yourself for a complete bathroom remodel, gutting it down to bare studs and subfloor. Major water damage causes problems beneath surfaces that must be repaired as soon as possible. If allowed to remain untouched, dry rot, mold, and mildew will continue to spread causing more and more problems as time goes by.

A surge in the number of active and ambitious do-it-yourself homeowners has prompted many companies to switch gears from catering strictly to professionals towards a more helpful approach for those novices who insist on tackling and completing their own home-improvement endeavors. Hence, the opening of more and more home-improvement centers staffed with experienced tradespeople and the in-depth, yet easy-to-comprehend, installation instructions included with all sorts of home-improvement products. Should you decide to remodel your own bathroom, plenty of help is available.

Depending on the nature and structural complexity of bathroom remodeling projects, homeowners can expect to save from 25 to 50 percent of the overall cost of hiring professional contractors by doing the work themselves. Indeed, you would be wise to hire professionals to complete intricate jobs that you haven't a clue how to complete, like major electrical, foundation, and plumbing work. Beyond that, you can install bathtubs, shower units, sinks, faucets, paint, wallpaper, floor vinyl, and the like to save money and gain self-satisfaction.

This book is designed for eager do-it-yourselfers with at least some knowledge of how hand and power tools are safely and efficiently operated, how homes are basically constructed, and how electrical and plumbing utilities are routed and designed to function. You must expect to spend time reading installation and operating instructions, and take time to thoroughly plan those jobs you have at hand in order to arrive at satisfactory results.

If you have limited experience working with tools, practice on scrap materials before attempting repairs or updates on those things you expect to install in a new pristine bathroom. Practice makes perfect and every professional I know has learned lots of lessons the hard way—by ruining beautiful pieces of wood or having to tear out inferior installations only to start all over again because of simple mistakes that could have been avoided if more time was taken for planning.

Taking your time, thinking jobs through before starting them, and asking pertinent questions at home-improvement centers will reward you with jobs well done, long-lasting results, and a great deal of self satisfaction. By the way, according to a report published in the newspaper not long ago, homeowners can expect to recoup an average of about 80 percent of bathroom remodeling costs when they sell their homes. Not a bad investment, especially if you get to enjoy new bathrooms for any length of time before selling your home.

Speaking of enjoyment, no do-it-yourself project has ever been enhanced by the experience of personal injury. Follow recommended operating instructions for all hand and power tools; wear safety goggles during every activity that entails the use of power, striking, or cutting tools; wear a dust mask or respirator during dust-causing activities; wear goggles and appropriate gloves when engaged in tasks dealing with harsh chemicals or rough materials; have a fire extinguisher handy during pipe soldering tasks; a first aid kit ready for any emergency; and, always shut off electrical power to those areas of your home involved with any type of electrical renovation—no matter how small.

Follow along and allow this book to show you how to prepare for and install all sorts of bathroom fixtures and accessories. One book cannot possibly include answers to every question so expect to compliment this one with the installation and operating instructions provided with your new bathroom fixtures and accessories. Patience, practice, and common sense will reward you with great looking, efficient, convenient, and satisfying bathroom remodeling endeavors.

Bathroom basics

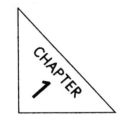

WITHOUT GOING INTO GREAT DETAIL, bathrooms are typically home spaces designed to deliver large amounts of clean water and dispose of water waste. A simple and convenient home amenity, perhaps, made possible by the use of pipes, faucets, drains, and specific fixtures. However, because wood, drywall, and other common construction materials cannot maintain their integrity under constant exposure to water, means of providing moisture barriers must be employed to keep bathrooms in structurally sound condition.

Bathrooms have to be outfitted in such a way as to control water flow, both directly through pipes and fixtures and indirectly through the venting of steam-laden atmospheres by way of fans and/or windows.

Beyond the basic requirements of providing clean water delivery and waste water disposal, bathrooms typically offer places where other types of personal hygiene takes place. If you are blessed with a family that includes children in their teenage years, you can sympathize with the fact that bathrooms require much more than just a water system.

Electrical outlets, mirrors, medicine cabinets, shelves, towel racks, toothbrush holders, and the like make bathrooms more efficient and convenient. With the addition of attractive wall and floor coverings, some pictures or plants, and other amenities, bathrooms easily can be designed to serve as useful and eye-appealing home attributes.

Bathroom storage

If your family is typical of most, chances are your bathrooms are chocked full of hair-care products, skin lotions, perfumes, deodorants, toothpaste, soap, and a host of other things.

A window ledge, plain plywood shelf unit, and medicine cabinet adequately serve as storage spots for a multitude of bathroom items. Although storage is functionally maintained, this bathroom is quite an eyesore. It would be visually enhanced by a finished shelf unit, preferably with doors, a larger medicine cabinet with additional storage capacity, and perhaps an attractive basket on the window ledge.

Vanity units are ideal for the storage of cleaning supplies, rolls of tissue, bars of soap, and so on. Along with that, drawers are most useful for the storage of small items, like hair ribbons, combs, and makeup.

Very similar to trays employed to keep silverware neatly arranged, the drawer tray from Häfele is designed for bathroom vanities. Numerous sizes are available to fit almost any vanity drawer. Use them to keep commonly needed items separated and easy to retrieve, while maintaining drawers in an organized condition. (Shown at top of next page.)

Almost every bathtub and shower unit would be well served with its own system of storage. Bars of soap, and containers of shampoo, hair conditioner, and other bathing products are slippery when wet. They easily fall off bathtub ledges and shower shelves when you try to put them back after use. An

easy solution is a simple bathtub and shower shelf or rack for accessories.

Shower shelves are commonly available in home-improvement centers, variety stores, and even some supermarkets. Many models are designed with self stick and waterproof adhesives that simply glue onto walls. Others hang from shower spouts and are equipped with suction cups to keep them steady.

Along with a vanity, larger medicine cabinet, and shelf unit over the toilet, the addition of an extra towel rack or ring, a set of coat hooks for bathrobes, and even an attractive basket on a wide vanity top for bars of soap will help to keep your bathroom organized and uncluttered.

Bathroom water problems

Although fresh water plays a vital role in sustaining us and our planet and is such a miracle fluid that provides countless attributes, it can also be enormously destructive. Floods and tidal waves are devastating, of course, but even small concentrations of water allowed to remain in constant contact with certain components will eventually destroy those materials' structural integrity. Allowed to linger uncontrolled, water damage will spread behind walls and under floors to eventually cause the rotting and dilapidation of structural framing members, like wall studs, sill plates, and floor joists.

A sure sign of bathroom water problems is indicated by peeling paint and failed caulking around an old window. These areas have not been subjected to direct water contact. Rather, their demise is attributed to constant exposure to steamy shower atmospheres that were not controlled with proper ventilation by way of an open window or bathroom fan.

Peeled paint must be chipped away. If the underlying surface is in good condition, it must be sanded, sealed with a primer, and then repainted. Old caulking must be removed, the area cleaned and then new caulking applied. After that, family members that use this bathtub must turn on the bathroom fan during their shower and then crack the window open afterward to completely ventilate the bathroom area and free it from an excessively moist atmosphere.

With the window removed, evidence of water damage is obvious along the lower-left window ledge. Poorly applied or failed caulking allowed water to seep into the space between the window frame and the tiled ledge. Prolonged exposure to moisture has ruined a large portion of the waterproof drywall, called *greenboard*, and has resulted in the growth of mildew and early signs of dry rot on wood members. (Shown top of next page.)

A tell-tale sign of water damage is highlighted by a loose tile at the bottom-lower corner of this shower unit. Cracked tile grout and/or failed caulking have allowed water to seep behind the tile. That water then adversely affected the drywall surface behind the tile, thus causing it to loosen up and fall away. The mastic used to secure tile to the wall did not fail, it was the actual drywall surface that finally disintegrated allowing both the tile and its adhesive mastic to loosen.

It is common practice to apply caulking to the corners and along the bases of tiled walls to enhance overall sealing efforts. Caulking served its purpose in the old shower, but a section of grout has definitely failed on the left vertical side of the bottom tile resting second left from the corner. Chances are very good that water has penetrated this space to cause underlying damage to the greenboard behind the tile and possibly to wood frame members nearby.

To repair this problem, grout and caulking must be cut and scraped away from around the effected tile. The tile should be carefully removed, and underlying surface inspected for damage. If a section of greenboard has been damaged, all tiles along the two bottom rows of this shower area must be removed, damaged greenboard cut out, and new greenboard installed before tile can be replaced and grouted.

This bathtub/shower was served with just a shower curtain. Water escaped from the corner of the bathtub through an opening between the shower curtain and tiled wall. A piece of plastic cove molding had been glued in place along the floor and partially up the wall. Continued exposure to puddled water that had seeped behind the cove molding finally resulted in this section of disintegrated drywall. It must be cut away and replaced. (Shown top of next page.)

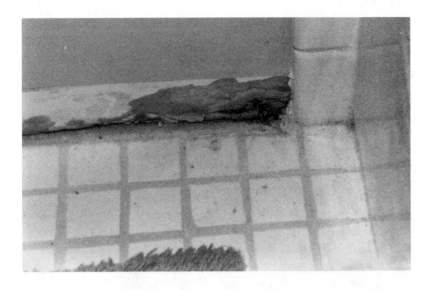

One of the easiest and most efficient means of containing water inside bathtubs and shower units is with quality shower doors. Chapter 8 discusses how to install both single shower unit doors and bypass bathtub models.

Water damaged bathrooms require repair. They have to be fixed before they fall apart. Reasons for their remodel are clear and simple. On the other hand, homeowners with bathrooms in good condition might want them remodeled as part of an overall home update or because they are ready for a change. In either case, homeowners are fortunate to have an exceptionally wide variety of quality bathroom fixtures available through home-improvement centers and local dealers.

Bathroom accessories

Because it might be difficult to select just the right sink, faucet, toilet, and bathtub combination from a catalog, Kohler Company offers help through a toll-free telephone number. By calling 1-800-4-KOHLER, you will be directed to the closest Kohler dealer in your area. Knowledgeable customer service staff will answer all of your questions and offer helpful tips on how to best install your new bathroom accessories.

New bathroom sinks and faucets can enhance almost any bathroom. Growing families might want to install two sinks to replace one older unit. The vanity shown is narrow; measuring only 18 inches from the wall to the front. Therefore, two Kohler Boutique Lavatory models were selected to accommodate a two-sink installation. Notice how the faucets are positioned at the corners making them compact and yet most functional. The units have been positioned close together for photo purposes only; they will be spaced apart proportionately along this 5-foot-long vanity top.

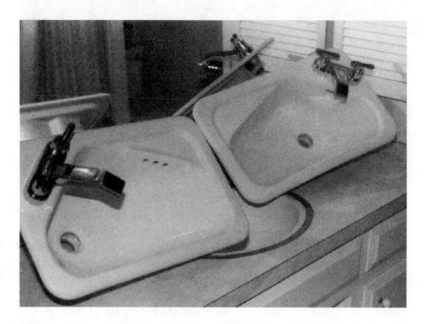

Bathroom lavatories (sinks) are available in all sorts of sizes, shapes, colors, and styles. Some are designed to rest on top of vanity tops, while others are mounted below to allow the rim of the countertop to actually serve as an actual lavatory top rim. The sink on the right offers ready-made holes for a faucet. The model on the left provides installers with options as to where they would prefer to mount a countertop faucet—in the middle or to the side for a unique effect. (See top figure of next page.)

Along with lavatories and faucets, bathtubs and showers are livened up with the new additions of bright faucets, spouts, and showerheads. (See bottom figure of next page.)

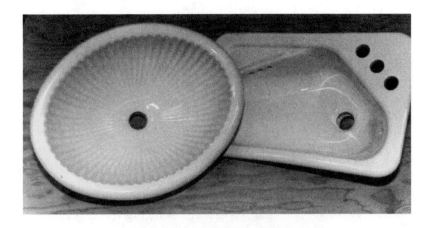

Because bathroom-fixture manufacturers employ their own special designs, not all bathtub/shower faucet handles will fit onto existing valves located just inside walls. This is an important consideration, especially if existing valves are in good condition. The only way to replace most single handle bathtub/shower valves is by cutting a hole in the wall behind the valve to gain access to the plumbing pipes that supply it. With water turned off and drained, pipes have to be cut in order to remove old valves. New sections of pipe are then soldered together to connect new valves.

New showerheads and spouts are installed from inside bathtubs and shower units. Although a little more work is involved with changing single bathtub/shower valves, you might prefer to do so to take advantage of the safety features built into Kohler's Rite-Temp valves.

Kohler's exclusive Rite-Temp pressure-balancing valves regulate the water pressure delivered to your bathtub or shower to eliminate surges of hot and cold running water when someone else turns on a faucet somewhere else in your home. In addition, these valves include an automatic anti-scald feature that shuts the water flow down should water pressure fail. A high temperature limit mechanism allows installers to preset maximum hot water temperatures as an added precaution. This is an especially ideal safety feature for young children.

In addition to a wide selection of various faucet, spout, and showerhead models, Kohler offers lots of accessory options. The polished brass showerhead is outfitted with a diverter valve that will cause water to flow through the body brush attachment. Shower units are typically served with a cold water pipe and a hot water pipe run to a valve. A third pipe goes from the valve to a threaded copper shower ell fitting. A shower arm or threaded copper pipe nipple is screwed into the ell at one end with a showerhead screwed onto the other.

If you are considering a complete new facelift for your bathroom, be prepared to spend time shopping for new fixtures and accessories. There are a lot of different styles, colors, and models to choose from, in polished chrome, polished brass, ceramics, and other materials.

Once you have all of your fixtures selected, consider a new medicine cabinet, light fixtures, wall covering, towel racks, and so on. Plumbing fixture dealers and home-improvement centers generally have numerous styles and models on display.

Be certain you do not overlook other basic bathroom necessities, like electrical supply and fan.

All bathroom electrical receptacles (outlets) must be protected by a Ground Fault Circuit Interrupter (GFCI). GFCIs react much quicker to abnormal electrical currents than common electrical panel circuit breakers. This is a major electrical safety concern for any outlet located near any water source, because water is a tremendous conductor of electricity.

In bathrooms, you could find yourself in trouble while using a faulty electrical device (such as a hair dryer) while standing in a small puddle of water. Electrical current escaping from a short in a faulty device would go through the user and immediately to ground provided by the water puddle. GFCIs are designed to immediately sense any such problem and shut the power off in an instant to prevent such accidental catastrophic electrocutions.

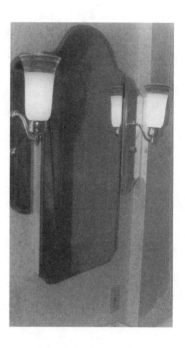

Bathroom designs

It is not always easy to arrive at a solid design for a complete bathroom remodel or brand new bathroom addition. There are many choices to make regarding fixtures and accessories, but what about selecting the actual locations for them?

Along with browsing through plumbing fixture dealer showrooms and home-improvement centers, consider the services of a National Kitchen & Bath Association certified bathroom designer. You might also enjoy good results working with a trained customer service representative from one of the large chains of home-improvement centers that offer computer-aided bathroom designing services.

Look through magazines, walk through open houses and model homes, talk to friends and neighbors who have remodeled their home's bathrooms, and so on. Ideas are plentiful; it is just a matter of finding and combining those special components and attributes that will make your bathroom remodel perfect for you.

Bathroom dimensions

Compacting too many bathroom accessories into spaces too small for them will not help your bathroom remodeling efforts. It is best to have accurate dimensional measurements of those fixtures you plan to install in your new or remodeled bathroom. The following might be used as a general industry-recognized guide:

- Half baths (toilet and sink only) require a minimum of 18 square feet.

- Three-quarter baths (shower stall) require 30 square feet minimum.

- Full baths (bathtub/shower) require a minimum of 35 square feet.

- Toilets generally measure 19 inches to 24 inches wide. Provide at least a 30-inch-wide space for them, with the center of the drain located a minimum of 15 inches away from each side wall.

- Toilets typically measure 27 to 30 inches deep and you should allow for at least 21 inches of clearance in front of them.

- Bathtubs range from 30 to 32 inches wide and 5 feet in length.

- Shower stalls are available in 30- by 30-inch sizes but 32 by 32 inches is about the smallest you would want to install. A stall 36 by 36 inches is a much more accommodating size. Provide at least 21 inches of clear walking space in front of both bathtubs and showers.

- Prefabricated vanities are available in 20 to 50 inch widths and 18, 21, and 24 inch depths. They generally sit 30 inches high.

- Leave at least 21 to 30 inches of free space in front of vanities.

- Plan for at least 24 inches of wall space width in front of lavatories.

- Leave from 2 to 6 inches open space from the edge of lavatories to side walls.

- Space two sinks no closer than 4 inches apart.

- Vanities for double sink installations should be at least 5 feet long.

Tools & materials

REGARDLESS OF HOW SMALL your bathroom remodeling project might be, you will need to employ tools of some kind. Some bathroom components require special tools, while most just call for the safe and efficient use of common hand and power tools.

Quality tools make a tremendous difference in how well home-improvement projects are completed. A cheap set of screwdrivers, for instance, will eventually frustrate you when their tips break or their fit is so bad that they strip out screwheads. A cheap wrench or socket will not grab tightly and it might strip the corners off of bolts.

Make sure all of your cutting tools are sharp; like saws, chisels, and razor knives. Rely on hand and power tools made by reputable manufacturers. They might cost a bit more; however, they will reward you with excellent performance and longevity. Always employ all tool guards and safety mechanisms with their positions properly adjusted for maximum efficiency.

Small repairs

A new coat of paint, floor vinyl, and some pretty plants might be all it takes to make your bathroom look fresh and revitalized. However, a toilet seat that frequently shifts unexpectedly or a unit that seems to flow water at all hours might be just enough to throw your bathroom update into a spin.

Toilet repair parts are commonly available at home-improvement centers, hardware stores, and plumbing dealers. Installation instructions are clearly printed on the back of packages or contained on sheets included with parts. It is best to note the type of toilet you are working on in order to retrieve the correct parts. For valves, pull off the top of the tank and look inside. See exactly what the fill valve, flapper, and float look like. By the way, the water inside toilet tanks is clean; the residue lurking along the bottom and sides is simply stuff that has settled over the years from the clean water supply. (See top of next page.)

Replacement toilet seat hinges are available in white plastic, chrome, and brass. They are easy to install with a flat-head or Phillips-head screwdriver. You might have problems removing old seat hinge screws that have become corroded. Clean off screwheads and ensure that the screwdriver fits tightly into the slots before attempting to remove them.

Hand tools

As you look at a bathroom lavatory, or any sink, from below and inside a vanity or counter, you might wonder how you are going to get a wrench on the bolts that hold faucets in place. Plumbers use a special tool that is commonly available wherever tools are sold.

A Shanknut wrench features a swivel head with a spring-loaded arm. A bar at the bottom allows users to turn the wrench while the head is in a horizontal position and grabs onto bolts. It is reversible, so you can use it for replacing bolts, too. To avoid stripping bolts, always attempt to screw them on as far as you can by hand, using the wrench only when bolts have tightened up. (Shown at top of next page.)

Individual hot and cold water bathtub and shower valves are secured in their mounting unit with large bolts, commonly referred to as *packing nuts*. Although removing entire valve bodies and replacing them with Rite-Temp balancing valves still requires an opening in the wall behind them, replacing leaky valve components is made from the bathtub or shower side. These special sockets are designed to fit particular valve packing nut sizes. After removing handles, simply place a socket on packing nuts, insert a screwdriver through holes at socket bases and unscrew.

Electrical power must be switched off at the circuit breaker or fuse whenever working on any electrical plug, receptacle, light fixture, and the like. To ensure correct circuit breakers have been switched off, use a tester like the one shown in the illustration. A small light in the tool's head will illuminate to signify the existence of live electrical power. If power has successfully been shut off, the light will not come on. Metal prods on the ends of the tool's wires make it easy to fit wires inside receptacles.

Power tools

Operated safely and in full accordance with manufacturer's instructions, power tools are capable of completing a tremendous amount of work in a fraction of the time it would take to complete identical tasks with hand tools. Likewise, haphazard and unsafe power tool usage could quickly result in ruined work and severe personal injury. Too much emphasis cannot be placed on the use of safety goggles and proper positioning of all tool safety guards.

For bathroom remodeling projects of any size, you will most likely need a power drill. A $\frac{3}{8}$-inch model is ideal for most drilling tasks. Along with the drill, you should have a full range of sharp drill bits. Various bathroom components require specifically sized drilling holes, such as a $\frac{7}{64}$-inch drill bit needed for one part of the installation of a Kohler Pipeline bypass shower door.

Professional remodelers regard reciprocating saws with the utmost respect. Tools like the Makita model are worth their weight in gold when it comes to demolition and remodeling activities. Metal cutting blades are used to cut through nails when trying to remove wall studs. Long bi-metal blades are employed for cutting away wood parts that might have nails in them. Be sure to use only those blades designed for the work you have at hand. Each blade package clearly defines the type of cutting tasks they are capable of achieving.

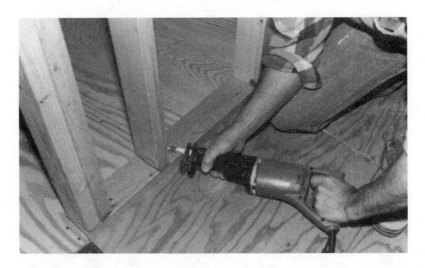

True do-it-yourselfers delight in completing home-improvement projects from beginning to end. Some even like to cut and mill their own wood. The Makita planer/jointer was used to turn a rough piece of oak dunnage into a beautiful and flawless vanity backsplash. Before it went through the planer/joiner a few times, had one edge routed with a round bit, was sanded, sealed, and stained, it looked just like the piece of rough oak dunnage next to it.

Along with making backsplashes out of rough lumber, you can also run those boards through a table saw to make vanity, cabinet, and shelf unit rails and stiles; you also can trim boards located on the fronts of such units. All of the rails and stiles for this new vanity came from oak dunnage materials, just like the backsplash. (See top of following page.)

The illustration shows the use of a Campbell Hausfeld Finish Nailer equipped with 1¾-inch nails to install a countertop trim rail. Notice that her left hand is placed in absolutely the worst possible position! Keep hands and fingers away from pneumatic nail guns to avoid any potential puncture injury. Also notice that for the purpose of this photo, the air supply hose was disconnected from the gun.

Another very handy finishing tool is the Campbell Hausfeld Brad Nailer. It shoots small nails that are perfect for window and door trim installations, moldings, and other small jobs. It is lightweight, compact, and rugged.

Every home-improvement job that entails the application of fine wood requires the use of a sander. Belt sanders are used for heavy sanding jobs, because they remove a lot of material in no time. Finishing sanders like the Makita model are commonly referred to as palm sanders. This is because they fit just right inside the palm of users' hands. A special plate outfitted with prongs is used to puncture sandpaper at precise locations in order for this tool to pick up a great deal of sanding dust and contain it in the cloth bag. After wood has been sanded to perfection, clean away all sanding dust and apply a quality sealer according to label instructions.

Victor Lopez, Technical Services Manager for the Behr Process Corporation, says that about 95 percent of all problems relating to paint and stain are a direct result of users failing to follow all recommended application instructions.

Years and years ago, before the advent of so many regulations over the use of chemicals, paints and stains were generally applied in all the same manner. Today, paint and stain manufacturers must follow strict rules governing the contents of their products and the processes by which they make them.

To conform to the rules and improve their products, chemists have developed specific quality products and methods for their application. This has resulted in better paints and stains that last longer and offer vividly wonderful hues. So if you want your paint and stain jobs to turn out as gorgeous as all of the paint and stain brochures you look through, be sure to read, comprehend, and follow all application instructions, especially those that refer to preparation work before the actual application of paint or stain.

Paint & stain

Water-based stains are becoming more and more popular. They are being developed to satisfy environmental concerns and also to make their application easier for users. The three products in the illustration are designed to work together, as designated on the back sides of their labels.

Bare drywall walls, all new wood, and most any other unpainted surface should be sealed before being painted or stained. Again, you must read label directions to be certain that the sealers you use are compatible with the paint or stain you plan to apply afterward.

Wall finishing

Brand new bathrooms, and those older ones that have been gutted down to bare studs, will have to be outfitted with new wall finishing materials. About the most common is drywall. Plan to install ⅝-inch-thick drywall on ceilings; its heavier nature does a good job of preventing sections located between ceiling joists from sagging. Drywall ½-inch thick is commonly used for walls.

Around bathtubs and shower units with tile walls, you could use greenboard. However, many professional contractors have found that those types of walls hold up better and last longer when finished with concrete backerboard. This heavy material combines Portland cement with fiberglass to produce an exceptionally water resistive wall base. Panels are commonly available in 3 by 5-foot sections, with some home-improvement centers carrying larger sheets.

Other than having someone else complete drywall work for you, about the easiest way to install drywall is with the PanelLift Telpro Drywall Lift. This remarkable tool rolls around easily on three heavy duty wheels and remains steady even while supporting a full sheet of ⅝-inch drywall next to the ceiling.

Drywall is typically installed on walls horizontally; with the 4 foot width extending from the ceiling down to midwall and the 8 foot or 12 foot length spanning from left to right along walls. Use the PanelLift for ceiling and upper wall drywall installation. You could purchase a unit for long term use on major home-improvement renovations or rent one from a rental yard for smaller jobs.

Bare drywall must be sealed before it is painted. Behr Undercoater is recommended for bare surfaces that will be coated with an enamel paint. A handy tip to prevent paint splatter while replacing paint lids is to make a number of small holes in paint can lid rims with a finishing nail. This way, paint that has gotten into the rim will drip back into the can, as opposed to being forced out all over the place while tapping lids secure with a hammer.

Because bathrooms are typically small, the addition of certain wallpaper styles might help to make it appear as if these rooms are actually larger. Wallpaper is available in all sorts of patterns, colors, and styles. Empire Brushes offers a complete wallpaper tool kit. It includes brushes, roller, razor knife, and string chalk line.

A small weight attached to the end of the string helps to maintain the string in a perfectly plumb (vertical) position. Chalk is first rubbed on the string. It is then held next to a wall at ceiling height with the weight located close to the floor. Once the weight stops moving and twisting, have someone else hold the string tight against the wall at floor level. Then, gently pull the string away from the wall and let it go. It will snap against the wall to leave a chalk line denoting a perfectly plumb line guide to which an edge of the first piece of wallpaper can be positioned against.

A brush with a handle is used to apply wallpaper paste to wallpaper. A wide brush is moved across wallpaper for smoothing and bubble removal. Use a little roller on wallpaper seams to help position them securely and remove any trapped air pockets.

The U.S. Ceramic Tile Company offers plentiful assortments of different wall, countertop, and floor tiles. Specific styles are arranged together in preset patterns to create three dimensional effects. Home-improvement centers and tile suppliers carry informational guidelines to help customers select the right kind of tiles for specific applications, like floors, around whirlpools, and so on.

Plumbing connections

Water supply pipes for bathtubs and showers are connected directly to faucet valves. Copper water pipes for toilets and lavatories are capped off just after they have been positioned to stick out of the wall. Once drywall has been installed, pipe caps are cut off and valves are attached to pipes before water is turned on.

PlumbShop offers handy vanity installation kits that include both hot and cold water valves, supply lines, and fittings needed to outfit vanity lavatories. The kit also includes a P-trap and drainpipe that extends from the base of lavatories to drainpipes that jut out of the wall.

Installation instructions generally are complete and easy to follow. Although your older bathroom might be in good overall condition, older shutoff valves might be on the brink of failure. Not so much that they might spring leaks, but they might not be capable of operating into the off position. This could be a disaster when a supply line is accidentally cut or faucet valve starts leaking and you are unable to shut off the water at the old valve. In that case, you would have to go out to your water meter or pump house and shut off the main water flow into your home.

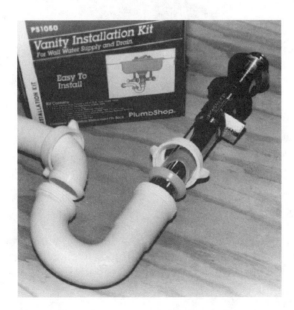

Bathroom illumination is important. Men need good light to conduct safe shaving operations and women must have sufficient light in order to apply makeup as they prefer. Although general overhead lighting is fine for most occasions, ideal bathroom lighting is obtained with vertical light bars

Lights & receptacles

placed on each side of vanity or medicine cabinet mirrors. Next best are light bars across the tops of mirrors.

Halo Lighting offers a number of different types and styles of recessed ceiling lights. The three recessed light housings are designed to support particular trim rings that fit inside and are the only things visible from inside rooms. Each housing and trim ring combination has certain limitations with regard to light bulb wattages. Because light bulbs get hot, it is important that wattage limits are not surpassed to prevent any problems with regard to excessive light fixture heat buildup.

Recessed light housings are simply nailed to ceiling joists and positioned along support rods. Ceiling drywall is cut only around the light's round opening to essentially hide the entire housing in the attic.

Because so much moisture is generated by the use of bathtubs and showers, specific types of recessed lighting units are required over them. The unit features an enclosed trim ring complete with a glass lens to prevent moisture from penetrating the unit and possibly corroding electrical connections. (See top of next page.)

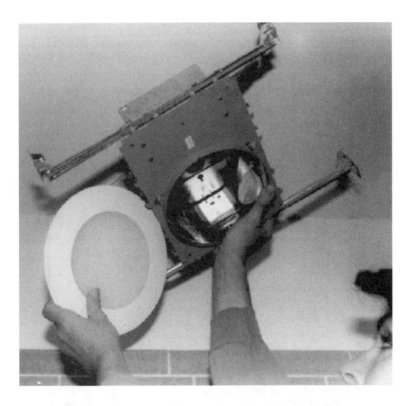

Along with special lights designed for use over moisture-laden areas, all bathrooms must be protected with a GFCI electrical outlet. GFCIs operate just like any other receptacle except that they can quickly sense abnormal current flows and shut off electrical flow in an instant. GFCIs are equipped with test and reset buttons. Once a month, you should push the test button and plug in a hair dryer or other electric appliance. With the test button activated, the electrical device should not operate. Press the reset button and the electric appliance should operate. Failure of this test means that the GFCI has failed and needs to be replaced.

Old vanities might look old, worn out, and dilapidated on the outside, but they could be structurally sound on the inside. For units in this condition, seriously consider refacing them.

Optional bathroom accessories

Quality Doors offers complete vanity, cabinet, counter, and cupboard refacing materials. These are just two of the many types of doors and one of several drawer front styles available. Hardware, like hinges and handles, are additional options. The units in the illustration are made of solid oak. They are top quality, heavy duty, and beautiful.

Along with doors, drawer fronts, and hardware, you can order rail and stile refacing materials to essentially change the entire appearance of almost any vanity. Doing the work yourself is very easy and will save a lot of money over the purchase of complete new vanity units. Before ordering materials and starting your project, contact Quality Doors and order a copy of their instructional videotape.

After you have remodeled your bathroom to perfection, take a moment to inspect door knobs or handles. Are they scratched, dulled, worn out, or ugly? Why not change them too?

Weiser Lock offers a wide variety of door handles, knobs, and locks for all installations. Bathrooms outfitted with polished

chrome accessories might be best served with chrome door handles. But what if the hallway or bedroom just off of the bathroom is decorated in natural wood and earth tones? Wouldn't a chrome handle on that side of the door look out of place? No problem. Weiser Lock offers door handle and knob units with a chrome handle on one side and brass on the other. Installation instructions are easy to follow and complete templates are included with each unit for installation into brand new doors.

CHAPTER 3

Bathroom dismantling

WALKING INTO AN OLD BATHROOM with a sledge hammer, crowbar, hard hat, gloves, goggles, and thoughts of dismantling everything in sight might conjure up pleasant thoughts for some folks. Especially if they have had to put up with annoying leaks, water stains, faulty fixtures, dim lights, broken vanity doors, and other inconveniences. However, this is not the prudent way to get started on any bathroom dismantling and remodeling project.

Using a sledge hammer to break up an old cast iron bathtub is appropriate. Why go through the hassle of jockeying it out of its stall when it is just headed for the refuse heap? But taking a sledge hammer to other bathroom components might result in more damage that will also have to be repaired; like pipes or wires inside walls.

Starting out

Gutting a bathroom down to bare studs results in a lot of debris that must be taken away to a refuse facility. So, before you begin, have a plan in mind as to how you are going to transport broken cast iron bathtub parts, wall tile, drywall, and floor covering material. (See top of following page.)

Turn off water supplies to sinks and toilets. When you are ready to take off the wall surrounding bathtub and shower faucets, turn off the main water supply at the water meter or pump house. Switch off the supply of electricity to the bathroom at its appropriate circuit breaker and check to ensure it is off completely by turning light switches on and off and plugging in an electrical tester to wall receptacles.

Wood trim around windows, doors, and vanities that is in good condition and just in need of paint or stain, should be taken off carefully. Use a flat pry bar to gently pull it away from the wall.

Finishing nails stuck in trim afterward should be pulled through the back of trim with a pair of side cutters or pliers. A hole will result in the front of trim but without splinters. You can fill those holes in later with putty, then sand and paint over them.

Most bathroom remodels do not require complete gutting. Generally, only small wall sections need to be stripped and rebuilt from the studs out. In these cases, you must control your dismantling efforts to prevent unnecessary damage and the need for additional repair work.

A new workshop has been constructed behind the first floor bathroom. This requires the removal of a bathroom window with its opening replaced with a solid wall. In lieu of tearing out all of the bathtub/shower tile and underlying wall surface that is in fine condition, work is concentrated only around the

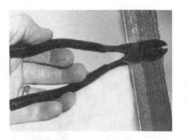

Tile removal & wall repair preparations

window opening. Finish work focuses on matching the tile color and pattern to make it look as though no window ever existed.

Taking a small sledge hammer to the tile around the window would surely result in cracked grout and tile away from the immediate work area. Therefore, a grout cutting tool is used to scrap away grout from the tiles surrounding the window opening.

Tiles placed along the window sides were secured with mastic. Although breaking them out by force was a consideration, it was thought best to remove them carefully to prevent any accidental damage to other tiles inside the tub enclosure. After grout was cut away from tiles, a heat gun was used to heat tiles and loosen mastic. A wide putty knife was slipped in behind tiles to pop them loose and pry them away from the wall.

Heat guns produce an incredible amount of heat. You must wear heavy leather gloves when working with these tools, because tiles will become too hot to touch with your bare hands. Also concentrated heat from one of these tools is strong enough to start combustible materials on fire! Beware that tool tips remain very hot for some time after tools have been shut off.

A larger amount of water damage was found than had previously been anticipated in the corner of the window. Notice how mildew spread from the lower ledge up the side of the stud, indicated by the dark spots on the wood. In addition, the greenboard in the area fell apart; moisture had just about disintegrated it.

Tile on the window ledge was secured with Thin Set Mortar—a cement-based product. This was done because of the amount of water that was expected to remain puddled on the ledge after showers were taken. Tile and thin set mortar were removed with careful use of a hammer and chisel.

Tiles around the inside perimeter of the window had to be cut in order to fit properly. In addition, greenboard along the perimeter edge was slightly water damaged. Therefore, tile grout was cut from around inside perimeter tiles and heat was used to slowly and gently remove tiles. This resulted in a suitable open work area where bad greenboard could be easily cut away and new greenboard installed. It also makes for a much easier and well blended new tile installation.

Installing new drywall or greenboard is always easiest when perimeter edges are cut clean and square. A pair of Quick-Grip bar clamps secure a metal straightedge that is used as a guide for the sharp razor knife. Because a full-sized header is located behind the window opening's top section, greenboard can be cut almost anywhere while leaving plenty of wood framing behind for the installation of new material. This is not always the case along window opening sides.

In almost all cases, only two studs are located on each side of window openings. On the inside, a cripple stud supports the end of the header. On the outside, a stud goes all the way up to the top plate. Therefore, if at all possible, try not to cut greenboard any further away than the cripple stud. This way, remaining greenboard is firmly secure to the outside stud while new greenboard can be nailed or screwed to the cripple.

If water damage has extended along greenboard past an outside window opening stud, you will have to install new 2×4s between that outside stud and the one to the side of it to provide backing support for the old greenboard remaining and new material to be installed. In this case, dismantling work would have had to continue all the way to the corner of the enclosure.

Vanity dismantling

Vanities are most often secured to walls with screws that go through a cleat at the back of units and into wall studs. In some cases, installers use nails instead of screws; however, screws are preferred. Vanity tops can be glued in place or attached to frames with screws from underneath. The illustration shows an inexpensive prefabricated vanity with a one-piece molded sink and countertop. Other types of vanities include separate countertops that should feature caulking along edges next to walls. Use a razor knife to carefully cut caulking before attempting to remove countertops.

Bathroom dismantling   33

Under the lavatory, turn off both the hot and cold water supply valves. Turn on the faucet to relieve water pressure trapped inside supply lines. Use a wide bucket to catch water that will drip out from the supply lines as they are loosened from the valves. In addition, place the bucket under the P-trap while hand tightened drainpipe fittings are loosened and disconnected. P-traps are designed to hold water in order to prevent sewer gas from passing through main drainpipes and out of lavatory drain openings.

The one-piece molded vanity top was simply glued to the top of the vanity frame. It was easily pulled up and away from the vanity once all piping was disconnected. (Below left.)

Some types of lavatories are secured in position on countertops with special clips; others are attached with sealant adhesives. To find out how existing lavatories are fastened, look at the bottom of them from inside the vanity. Clips are generally held in place with screws. (Below right.)

If the bathroom lavatory you are dismantling fits clearly over the edge of countertops, you should have no worry about the unit falling through the hole and onto your head while working underneath it. However, some types of vanities that rest flush with countertops and are adorned with a metal ring around them could fall through. As you loosen sink clips, keep one hand firmly on lavatories to prevent them from falling. Better yet, have a helper assist you by holding onto units from the top through drain holes, faucets, or overflow openings.

Had screws been used to secure the vanity to the wall, no amount of prying would have been needed. The installation of nails, however, requires pry bar efforts. To avoid poking prying tools through existing drywall, place a board behind them at their fulcrum point. Notice that a piece of plastic that was secured with a water pump clamp over the open drainpipe stub. It will prevent sewer gas and possibly waste water from other home drains from flowing out.

As you can see, the tile floor was installed after the vanity. Although this vanity is cheaply made with thin materials, the front frame of rails and stiles are in good shape and there is no way a wider unit could fit into the cramped space. Because there

is room for a 24-inch-deep unit (this one is 18 inches), a new unit will be made utilizing the front frame that is simply held onto the sides with small staples. In addition, a piece of wood will be secured to the right side to cover a wasted opening caused by an 8-inch-high foundation wall. That piece of wood will be secured to the side of the front frame with wood biscuits and glue.

Mirrors & medicine cabinet removal

Mirrors and medicine cabinets are heavy. They must be secured to walls with wood screws that penetrate into studs by at least one inch. Various types of mirrors and cabinets are held in position with different kinds of clips. Look first for screws and loosen them slightly, just enough for you to move the unit a bit to see how it is secured all around.

It is obvious that screws were not used to secure the top of the unit. Two screws were located inside the sliding doors. After the unit was completely empty and obstacles removed from in front of it, the screws were loosened enough to allow a peek behind the mirror. It was then discovered that a rail attached to the back of the mirror was resting inside two metal clips screwed to the wall.

Realizing that the mirror cabinet would not fall down once the screws inside the doors were taken out, work continued. The unit was lifted up and out of the clips, moved to another location, and remodeling work continued.

Because the old bathtub/shower valve and handle are scheduled to be replaced with a new Rite-Temp valve and attractive Kohler handle, work will continue on the backside of this wall behind the bathtub to cut a hole in the wall and remove the old bathtub/shower valve. After that, greenboard and drywall work will commence. While drywall mud cures, efforts can be concentrated on building a new vanity unit.

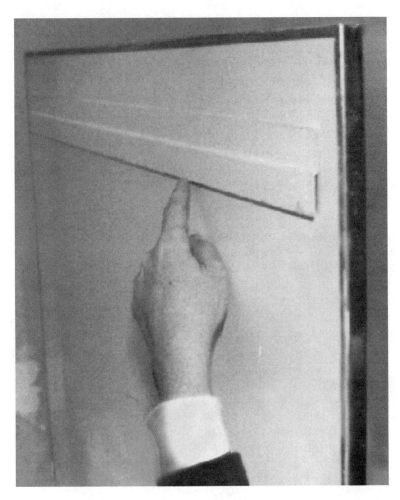

CHAPTER 4

New construction

MANY of the factors that go into building new bathrooms for new homes and additions are every bit as important for old bathrooms completely gutted down to bare studs and subfloor. Before getting too carried away with thoughts of quickly finishing the rough-in work to get to the drywall and finishing tasks, take plenty of time to consider what other types of amenities you might want to install before all of the walls are covered up.

Such examples might include an exterior light for a rear or side yard located next to the project bathroom. Electrical wiring and fixture boxes must be installed. How about an electrical outlet for the yard off of the bathroom's exterior wall? It must be GFCI protected and not part of the separate bathroom electrical circuit. A new outdoor water spigot, perhaps? In areas that experience cold winter temperatures, be certain to install a freeze-proof spigot and insulate pipes.

Initial concerns

The best way to prevent squeaky wood floors is to secure subfloor material to floor joists with subfloor adhesive and deck screws.

Knee pads are excellent options while working on floors. The Makita drill/driver combined with a finder/driver works great for quickly installing lots of deck screws; be sure to wear safety goggles! Janna is demonstrating how a sheath on the finder/driver slides over screws to hold them in place on the magnetic tip while preparing to drive screws. (She will don her safety goggles before actually getting started.) (See following page.)

For the construction of new bathrooms and extensive remodels where bathrooms are scheduled for enlargement, you might get a better perspective of the initial plans by placing boards where you believe walls should be built. The new bathroom will feature a whirlpool toward the left under the three windows, a double lavatory vanity in front of the black drain vent pipe in the center, a toilet space under the window to the right, and a

3- by 5-foot double shower in the projection at the lower-right corner of the photo. (See top of following page.)

A great amount of time was spent deciding where to locate the door into this bathroom and how wide it should be. First thoughts focussed around double-raised panel pocket doors. But a required service opening through the wall at the whirlpool location thwarted that idea. (See bottom of following page.)

40 Bathrooms: Remodeling projects

Another option was a single pocket door extending toward the right, but that would have hindered the ability to hang towel racks next to the shower, because pocket doors are framed with thin material to provide an opening inside the wall for the door. It was finally agreed that a 2-foot-8-inch door would be installed in the center of the bathroom and open to the right toward the shower stall.

The partition wall between the master bedroom and bathroom was constructed with 2×4 studs on 16-inch centers. Because it will support only its own weight, it features a single top plate. Built and raised into position and wedged against the roof/ceiling trusses, it was maneuvered next to a chalk line already made on the floor.

A string was tied to nails driven part way into both ends of the bottom plate and chunks of 2×4 placed between the bottom plate and string. A third chunk of 2×4 was then used as a measuring gauge. The bottom of the wall was tapped to one side or the other at different points where it did not rest in a perfectly straight line, as determined by the 2×4 gauge placed between it and the string. Once the wall was maneuvered into a straight line, it was secured to floor joists with 16d nails.

A level was used to determine the wall was plumb before the top was secured to the trusses with 16d nails. Framing in windows will not generally require the use of string guides and levels. For a repair like this to blend in with the existing wall, you have to install framing flush with its surroundings, even if the entire wall is out of plumb. To set this window opening framing perfectly plumb and not flush with the outer frame would cause a multitude of problems when it came time to blend new tile with old.

Floor underlayment & utility access

All plumbing drainpipes must be installed and inspected by the local building inspector before concrete floors are poured. You must pay strict attention to bathtub, shower stall, whirlpool, and toilet installation instructions to locate waste pipes in their proper position. Once concrete is poured, it is too late to relocate those waste drains. In addition, you must provide your bathroom vanity wall with a drainpipe through the floor if it will not be within close proximity to the main waste drain stack.

For the most part, subfloors consist of ¾-inch tongue and groove plywood designed specifically as subfloor material. Sheets are placed on top of floor joists and spaced about ⅛ inch apart to compensate for expansion and contraction. Fifteen-pound building paper is rolled out on top of it and then covered with ½-inch plywood or underlayment-rated particleboard.

Be certain all subfloor areas are swept clean before rolling out building paper. In addition, you should take care of other flooring concerns before actually stapling paper into place.

Shower pans must be provided with a drain hole in the floor. Installation instructions provide exact measurements for these access points. In this case, a wall was left free in order to accommodate the physical insertion of the shower pan. Had the wall been secured in place, it would have been difficult if not impossible to get the pan in there. While it was there, a simple pencil line was drawn around the drain hole to designate where to cut a floor opening.

Access must also be provided for toilet waste pipes. Toilets require a minimum 3-inch waste pipe. A plastic cover has been glued to the pipe opening to prevent sewer gas from escaping into the area and also as a means to hold water during the new construction piping wet test. Once the closet flange is secured over it with ABS plastic glue and the toilet is ready for installation, the plastic cover will be broken out.

Heat ducting is another concern. You must provide openings in floors for registers. A pencil line was made around the perimeter of this boot and small holes drilled in the corners. Nails were inserted into those holes and an inspection was made in the room below to ensure there would be no problems in locating the duct at that point.

Back at the shower drain, a single hole was bored in the center of the drain location. From deck screw locations on top of the subfloor, it was easily determined that a floor joist was not in the way. However, an inspection was made below to ensure no problems would be encountered with a shower drain installed at this location.

The shower pan installation instructions called for a 6- by 6-inch access hole for the drain. That dimension was drawn out on the subfloor positioned around the pencil line made through the actual pan's drain opening. The circular saw was set to cut at a depth of about 1 inch and then carefully lowered down onto the lines one at a time. Cuts were made just up to intersecting lines and not past them. A handsaw was employed to finish the cuts.

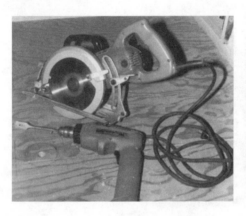

Once you roll out building paper onto the subfloor and place ½-inch underlayment on top, it is difficult to determine the locations of floor joists and where deck screws should be inserted. Therefore, draw pencil lines on top of adjacent wall bottom plates to show where joists are positioned.

Because building paper and underlayment are installed pieces at a time, it is easy to snap chalk lines from these markings over to subfloor areas where the deck screws remain clearly evident. Then you can insert deck screws along those chalk lines made on underlayment.

As with subfloors, underlayment should feature ⅛-inch gaps between walls and adjacent sheets. The easiest way to ensure ⅛-inch gaps is to drive 8d nails partly into subfloors along underlayment sheet perimeters. The 8d nail is about ⅛ inch in diameter.

Although it might be easier to cut drain and heat register access holes after underlayment has been installed, there might be times when you need to ensure their correct position before underlayment chores have begun. When that's the case, guarantee that holes in underlayment line up with those in the subfloor by initiating the work from below. The illustration shows how building paper is cut away from the shower drain hole with a razor knife.

Ensured that nobody and no obstacles are located directly above the access hole, drill holes in all four corners. These holes will

serve as guides above for cutting. In lieu of this method, simply drill a wide hole big enough for a reciprocating saw blade to fit through and cut the hole from underneath.

Newer building codes include specific insulation regulations. Different regions are required to install insulation of various R-values. In the Pacific Northwest, attic spaces are insulated with R-30 material and walls must be insulated with R-21. Check with your local building department to learn of the requirements in your area.

Insulation

The Eagle casement window has been sealed and insulated with expanding foam. The material exits a spray can through a tube as a thick sticky paste. Over the course of a few hours, it expands to around three to four times in size. Cut off excess dry material that spreads out past window jambs with a razor knife.

Not all windows or doors are designed to withstand the effects of expanding foam. The nature of their construction could cause trim to bow inward as foam expands. Before applying expanding foam around your windows, check with your window representative to ensure such applications are suitable.

Owens-Corning offers pink insulation in different R-values with paper moisture barriers on one side, plain with no moisture barriers, and encapsulated in a plastic barrier. The R-30 ceiling batts are 9½ inches thick, 24 inches wide, and 4 feet long. They snugly fit between roof trusses spaced 2 feet on center and their short length makes them easy to manage during insulation. Flaps on both sides fold out and are stapled to the bottom of trusses or ceiling joists.

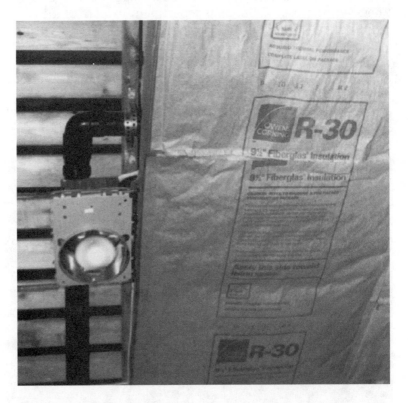

Insulation installers should wear long sleeve garments, gloves, safety goggles, and a dust mask or respirator. Insulation batts are cut with a sharp razor knife. It is easiest to cut through the paper moisture barrier first and then through the fiberglass material.

At the ceiling and next to the drain vent pipe, notice holes in the wood just above the wall's top plate. These are screened attic ventilation holes made in the blocks that are positioned between the roof trusses. They must not be blocked by

insulation. Therefore, cut away a portion of insulation at these ends to accommodate an unobstructed airflow through vents. Employ numerous light cuts with a sharp razor knife to carefully cut away insulation material. (See illustration above.)

Insulation must be made to fit around pipes, electrical boxes, and other obstacles. You might find it easiest to place batts on top of a piece of plywood resting on sawhorses and use accurate measurements to determine where insulation backsides must be cut in order to fit around things. During actual installation, reach into and pull batt material apart to make way for pipes and then maneuver insulation around pipe backsides. (See illustration on following page.)

Drywall

Sheets of drywall are not nearly as rigid as plywood. Therefore, use caution when carrying and setting sheets down. Knocking them into walls will dent or crack edges and they could crack in half when simply supported at one end. Handle drywall from the center; better yet, have a helper assist you in maneuvering sheets.

Drywall can be nailed in place to studs with special drywall nails. They are galvanized and feature a cupped head. Drive them partially into drywall creating a slight dent. Drywall

mud will then be troweled over dents to fill them and cover nail heads.

In lieu of nails, most installers prefer to use drywall screws. They are installed much quicker and easier. Although a drill/driver might be employed to drive drywall screws, it is best to use an actual drywall screw gun. These power tools feature an adjustable tip mechanism that guarantees every screw will be driven into drywall at the same depth.

Fiberglass shower stalls are equipped with flanges around their outside edges and along the top. Holes must be drilled through these flanges before nails or screws are inserted. If not, fiberglass could crack. While installing greenboard drywall around fiberglass stalls, be sure to drill through greenboard and the stall flanges before driving drywall screws. Strips of masking tape designate where screws have already been placed to secure the shower stall. (See top of following page.)

A small hole the size of a drywall screw shank was first drilled through greenboard and the shower stall flange only with an angle drill. That operation was followed by the installation of drywall screws with a drywall screw gun.

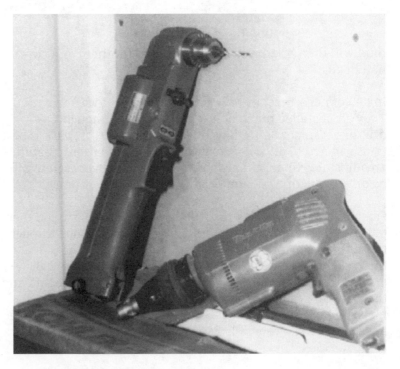

Drywall seams, inside and outside corners, and all nail or screw heads are covered with joint compound, most commonly referred to as *drywall mud*. Seams and inside corners are coated with mud first and then covered with drywall tape, a paper material. Then, another layer of mud is spread over the tape to keep it in place. Outside corners are initially covered with a piece of corner bead; a metal strip shaped at a 90-degree angle and secured with nails or screws.

Drywall is generally treated to three coats of mud; however, just one tape application is required. Apply the first mud coat with a trowel or putty knife about 5 to 6 inches wide. Allow mud to cure for 24 hours or until all dark spots have cured to the same light color as surrounding dry edges. After mud has adequately dried, use a bigger trowel, about 8 inches wide, to scrape away excess mud and then apply a second wider coat. Next, knock off excess mud with a trowel. Use a 12-inch-wide trowel to apply the third and final coat of mud.

If you look closely at sheets of drywall and greenboard, you'll notice that the paper covered edges are tapered; they bend down toward the edge. These edges should be installed next to each other and the open ends butted against one another. This ensures either a complete tapered joint or a flat one.

Using wider and wider trowels enables you to spread drywall mud smoothly to form an eventual flat layer. You won't be able

to shape flat and level drywall joints with trowels. Do the best you can but opt for too much mud rather than too little.

The final phase of drywall finishing entails lots of sanding. This is where perfection will take place. If enough mud has been applied, you will have plenty of material to work with. If your applications were too sparse, sanding could reach down to actual drywall and mar the actual drywall paper, which is not good. To help drywall finishers do a good job of sanding, Stanley-Goldblatt offers a number of drywall sanding tools. Along with a hand-held block, a swivel model is available that attaches to a pole; it is ideal for ceiling and upper-wall sanding jobs.

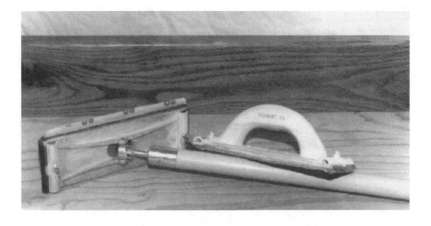

Sanding drywall mud will create an amazing mess. Resulting sanding dust is very fine and will filter into all home areas. Plan to seal off bathrooms with sheets of plastic and masking tape and then be certain to wear safety goggles and a dust mask or respirator while sanding. Before attempting any drywall or greenboard sealing work, be sure to clean away all sanding dust debris. A powerful wet/dry vacuum will be most helpful.

The label on DAP Wallboard Joint Compound suggests that drywall mud sanding can be best achieved by the use of a water dampened sponge. This process works very well and eliminates the hassles related to sanding dust. Especially for small drywall sanding jobs, this process is excellent.

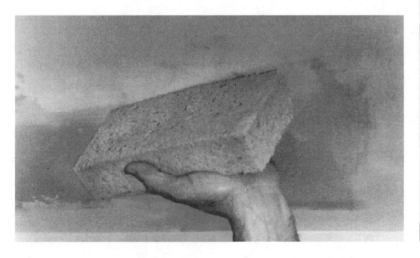

Once drywall has been completely sanded to perfection, you might choose to coat ceilings and walls with a texture coat, also referred to as *knock down*. Tools and equipment used for this process are readily available at tool rental yards and some home-improvement centers. Basically, these devices spray on a product very similar to drywall mud but in globs of various textures. Some are left as is and others are knocked down flat with a trowel. Bathroom ceilings should not be adorned with thick popcorn textures, because moisture will cause them to fall away.

Plumbing

AS REFERRED TO EARLIER, the main difference between bathrooms and other parts of most homes is the requirement for large volumes of fresh water supplies and the disposal of waste water. This situation mandates one system that brings in both fresh hot and cold water and another to drain away all waste.

The theory behind plumbing is easy. Fresh water is supplied through a metropolitan system where water flows under pressure supplied by pumps at numerous pumping stations strategically located throughout regional areas. Waste water flows downhill by the force of gravity until reaching a point where pumping stations force the material to sewage plants.

For people living in rural areas, fresh water is supplied by a pump that brings fresh water out of wells. Waste water again flows downhill by the force of gravity and into septic tanks for holding and eventually into drain fields under the ground close by.

In both cases, waste water systems, referred to as *Drain-Waste-Vent Systems* (DWV), are equipped with vent pipes that extend up and out through roofs. These pipes provide DWV systems with balanced atmospheric pressure to prevent draining waste from one fixture from sucking out the water in P-traps from others and exposing home interiors to sewer gas. It also helps waste to flow smoothly and quickly through drainpipes.

Fresh water is supplied to homes by a 1-inch main line. It is then tapered down into a ¾-inch line for the long stretches to remote home locations. All piping and connections at use sites are completed with ½-inch pipe.

Located in the exterior of the new bathroom 2×6 wall are two copper pipes and a single DWV pipe. The setup is typical for a single lavatory arrangement. In this case, a double lavatory is desired. Therefore, additional fresh hot and cold water copper pipe will be installed along with a redesigned DWV system. The

Setting up your bathroom's plumbing system

main DWV pipe will remain in place, as it attaches to a main 2-inch drain line that runs to a 3-inch main stack and then into a large 4-inch-underground residential sewer line. It also extends up into the ceiling and connects with the main stack for proper venting. The following will help you determine what size drainpipe you will need:

- Vanities require a 1½-inch drainpipe.
- Showers and bathtubs require a 2-inch drainpipe.
- Toilets require a 3-inch drainpipe.
- Main sewer drains must be 4 inches.

Plumbing regulations vary among different regional areas with regard to DWV systems. Some require venting at every fixture and others rely on various distances from vents before requiring additional vents. Check with your local building department before starting any new construction to ensure you abide by all local building codes. With regard to remodeling, simply employ existing drains and vents unless you have experienced problems with slow draining fixtures or other problems.

While planning your plumbing tasks, draw out designs on a piece of paper. This will help you determine how many of which kinds of fittings you'll need. If you are like most everyone else, buy more than you expect to need because undoubtedly your job will require more than expected. Home-improvement centers are loaded with 90-degree and 45-degree elbows, Ts, 4-way fittings, and everything else plumbers require.

Drill holes and position pipes loosely until all connections have been routed and fitted together. Do not permanently glue ABS plastic DWV pipe together or solder copper pipe until you have completely assembled your plumbing grid. This way you can easily make changes without having to unravel all of the work previously completed.

Both fresh hot and cold water lines have been loosely assembled. Notice the holes in studs on both sides of the DWV pipe. During copper pipe routing, ABS drain lines were placed in position so that copper pipe routing could be gauged. Horizontal copper pipe bracket supports must be slipped onto nipples before caps are soldered on. They will not fit over caps. (See top of following page.)

Copper pipe extensions rising above the horizontal pieces extending through the potential covered wall are designed as

water hammer dampeners. Trapped air in them will suppress
the sudden closing of faucets to reduce the noise and damage
created by water hammering effects.

A hole saw attached to a Makita ½-inch angle drill works quickly to bore holes in studs for ABS plastic DWV pipe. The small metal plate located next to the cold water copper supply pipe on the right is a nailing plate. It will be attached to the stud as a means to prevent drywall nails or screws from penetrating through the stud and into the pipe located closer than 1½ inch from the inside face of the stud.

Routing drain vent pipes can sometimes be a problem, especially when installing new bathrooms in existing homes. On the left, a new 2-inch-black ABS plastic vent pipe has been connected to an existing vent pipe that extends up to the roof. A tee was installed in the existing pipe and was then outfitted with an elbow. A short section of straight pipe was glued to it and then connected to another elbow from the new pipe. Notice the short strips of white tape attached in the center of this connection. They were placed during the initial setup to ensure that once glue was applied, they would be joined together at the proper angle.

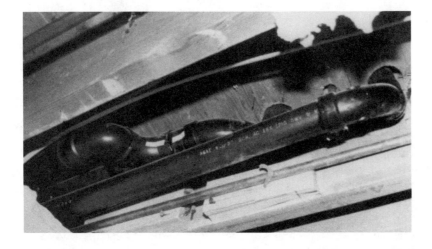

ABS plastic DWV pipe and its connections must be secured with glue specifically designed for ABS materials. This glue sets very fast; you only have a few seconds for final adjustment.

All pipe must be securely anchored to structural frame members. The illustration shows a vent pipe held in place with metal strap nailed to a roof truss member.

Especially for new construction, all DWV piping must be tested under water pressure. This is accomplished by inserting an inflatable test plug into a cleanout or test tee located at the base of the system. Water is then flowed from a garden hose into the vent pipe that extends out of the roof. Building officials will inspect all DWV piping to ensure no leaks occur. This ensures that waste leaks and sewer gas will not escape into living areas. (See top of following page.)

The test plug is inserted into piping and then filled with air or water; extensions are available to accommodate this endeavor. Removing test plugs is another matter—expect to get wet. Never stick your hand into a test tee to remove a test plug. Water pressure from above could easily cause broken fingers or

hands. Use a long screwdriver to release air pressure inside the device and then pull on the chain to remove it.

Cut copper pipe to length with a pipe cutter. Pipe cutters feature an adjustable shank equipped with a wheel located beneath a cutting head. They are also equipped with a pointed knife-like projecting arm that is used to deburr interior pipe edges. Of great assistance for most all plumbing jobs is a handy fitting container from the Plano Molding Company.

For solid connections, solder fresh water copper pipes and fittings together. You will need emory cloth and a wire brush tool to properly clean the surfaces of all components, flux to coat all connections, a roll of solder, and a torch. Before starting out on your bathroom's plumbing needs, practice with a few pieces of pipe and fittings first. You will be amazed at how easy and simple it is to solder copper pipe and fittings together.

Clean copper pipes with emory cloth and brighten interior fitting surfaces with a wire brush. Be certain all surfaces are cleaned to a brilliant shine to ensure against inadequate soldering joints. (See top of following page.)

Soldering copper pipe

Once pipe ends and fittings have been cleaned, apply a liberal amount of flux to them with a small brush. Most home-improvement centers offer kits that include flux and brushes.

Heat from a propane torch is focussed on fittings, not pipe. Once flux starts to boil and smoke, pipe has just about been heated enough to melt solder. When pipe has been heated to just the right temperature, solder will instantly melt and be drawn into the connection. (See top of following page.)

For all practical purposes, expect to use a ½ inch of solder for joining ½-inch-pipe connections; ¾ inch of solder for connecting ¾-inch pipe and fittings; and 1 inch of solder for 1-inch pipe. In

this case, too much is not too good. Excess solder will just drip away to make a mess.

When soldering fittings onto pipe ends, be sure fittings are positioned above pipe at an upward angle. This will prevent excess solder from flowing through interior areas and onto threads or other interior surfaces machined to accept only specified diameter pipe sizes.

The 90-degree joint soldered together on the top displays a lot of excess soldering material. It is a sloppy job. The threaded fitting on the bottom has been nicely accomplished.

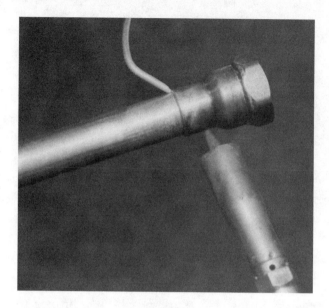

Immediately after completing soldering operations on a fitting, apply a sopping wet rag to the connection to clean away excess solder and cool the joint. Be extremely careful while conducting this operation, because pipe and fittings will be dangerously hot. Hot soldering operations have been responsible for many structural fires. Heat from a torch will easily catch wood framing members on fire. To ensure overall plumbing safety, locate a flameproof pad behind soldering operations to protect wood members and other objects that could be damaged by torch flames. (See top of following page.)

Heat generated by copper pipe soldering can cause problems with various plumbing components, like Rite-Temp balancing shower valves. A means to prevent any accidental damage to valves is to first solder on fittings to pipe. Then wrap the male threads of the valves with Teflon pipe tape and attach fittings. Secure valves in position with nails or boards and wrap a sopping wet rag over the pipe while soldering the pipe end to an elbow or coupling connection. (See bottom of following page.)

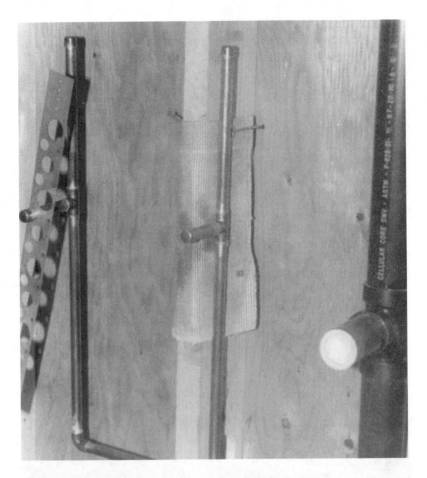

By conducting actual soldering operations away from valves and with the application of a wet rag between them, you will essentially protect valves from all effects of heat generated by your soldering torch.

Fresh water pipe testing & securing

Building inspectors will want to see your fresh water system tested before approving the installation. This is accomplished by way of air pressure and an air pressure gauge.

Somewhere in your fresh water pipe system, you must install an air pressure gauge equipped with an air inlet valve, like a tire stem. These units are available at home-improvement centers and plumbing supply outlets. Hot and cold water lines can be interconnected with flexible copper lines like those used for hot water heaters. Be sure that all open pipe ends are capped off with caps soldered in position. These are generally those stubs that stick out of walls and are expected to support valves for lavatories and toilets.

Air pressure from a compressor is introduced into the piping system at a pressure from 80 to 100 psi. The system must maintain this pressure for a minimum of ten minutes. If it drops, you have a leaky connection.

About the best way to locate stubborn piping leaks is with a mixture of rich soapy water and a paintbrush. Escaping air will cause soapy solutions to immediately and noticeably bubble up. Notice the nailing plate located on the stud in front of the copper pipe. Nailing plates will save you trouble by protecting all pipes and electrical wires located closer than 1½ inches to the face of studs. Just imagine the dilemmas that could be caused by holes in pipes or shorts in wires discovered only after all drywall and finishing tasks have been completed.

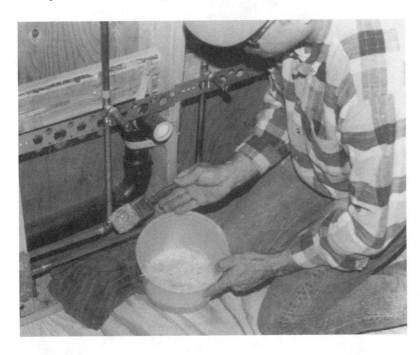

Satisfied that all of your fresh water piping has passed the pressure test, proceed to secure all pipes to framing members. A variety of devices are readily available at home-improvement centers and plumbing outlets designed to secure pipes to the holes bored inside studs, along the inner sides of wall studs, and in other places. Both an angle drill/driver and regular drill/driver were employed to secure plastic pipe supports to studs with Simpson Strong-Tie stainless steel screws.

This is a fine setup for a double lavatory vanity. The job is neat and tidy. Drainpipes for lavatories are generally set at about 18 inches off of the floor. Fresh water pipes are set slightly higher, around 21 inches. Notice the wood blocks behind piping positioned for pipe support and the nailing plates located in front of horizontal pipe supply lines.

Along with routing plumbing pipe supplies in an organized and systematic series, you must position components according to manufacturers' recommendations. Of primary importance are Rite-Temp balancing valves for bathtubs and showers.

A plastic shield screwed onto the valve indicates maximum and minimum clearances between the finished wall surface and the actual valve. This is an important concern, because the valve handle should securely engage with the valve to ensure the handle operates water flow appropriately. If the valve is placed too far into walls and away from handles, you will not be able to turn water on or off. If it is placed too close to the wall surface, the handle assembly will sit away from the wall and allow water to easily penetrate the wall cavity.

This is a threaded collared shower ell. The collar has been secured to a block of wood with screws, and a plug has been covered with a layer of Teflon sealant tape and screwed into the fitting. This is a typical rough plumbing application. The plug seals off the fitting to satisfy testing needs and will also keep drywall debris out of the fresh water system. Once all drywall work has been completed, a ratchet and socket can be used to remove it. (See top of following page.)

At that time, a showerhead arm will have its threads covered
with Teflon pipe tape and then be screwed into this secured
fitting. A shim of wood has been placed between the ell and
block of wood as a means to keep the pipe in a plumb position.

Finally, ensure against water pipes freezing by insulating them.
This is especially important in northern climates where winter
temperatures fall exceedingly low. Cylindrical foam pipe
insulation materials feature a lengthwise slit. This enables
installers to quickly pull them apart and place them over pipes.
Use a sharp razor knife to cut them to length.

CHAPTER 6

Electricity

THE ELECTRICAL NEEDS for most bathrooms are quite simple. They usually include: one electrical receptacle near a vanity; an overhead light or a fixture above a mirror or medicine cabinet; a fan; and possibly a wall mount heater.

To provide maximum personal safety while using any electrical device near a water source, electrical receptacles must be protected by a GFCI. In addition, that GFCI receptacle must be on a circuit that serves only bathroom receptacles; no lights and nothing else in the home. One circuit can serve all home bathroom receptacles as long as the very first receptacle served out of the electrical panel is a GFCI. Because all electrical current used on that circuit will first pass through that GFCI, following receptacles will also be protected.

Failure to abide by specific electrical codes and installation practices could result in fire or electrocution, so you are encouraged to seek the assistance of a qualified electrician whenever you engage in major electrical renovations or when posed with problems you do not know anything about.

Roughing-in

Electrical light switches, receptacles, and light fixtures are mounted to boxes that are nailed to wall studs. A number of different box sizes and shapes are available for all applications.

The best time to install electrical boxes is while walls are opened up to bare studs. In this case, a box for an outside light has been mounted near the ceiling next to an 8-foot wood framed sliding glass door. The switch for this light is mounted 4 feet from the floor and also next to the door. Electric wire will run into the switch box and then up to the light. (Shown at left.)

Electrical boxes should be mounted so that their front edges stick out past wall studs. On walls, they should be positioned so that the front sticks out ½ inch. This way, boxes will meet flush with the surface of drywall panels after they have been

installed to serve as a solid base for the ears on receptacles and switches when they are mounted inside boxes. For ⅝-inch drywall applications, mount boxes so that their front edge sticks out about ⅝ inch.

Electricity is measured according to current flow and volume; amperes (amps) and voltages (volts). Bathroom receptacles are served with 120-volt 20-amp circuits, while lights are generally served with 120-volt 15-amp circuits. Some wall heaters might require a 240-volt 30-amp circuit.

Electrical wire is available in different sizes on rolls from 50 feet to 250 feet. Cable designated 12/2 with ground means the cable is filled with three 12-gauge wires: one will be covered with a white coating (neutral), another will be black (hot), and the third will be bare (ground). Cable designated 14/2 with ground

Electrical wire

ground also includes three wires that are smaller, only 14-gauge. Cable designated 14/3 with ground has four wires: white, black, red, and bare ground. It is used for three-way light switch connections where two separate light switches operate a single light or a set of light fixtures.

Wire that is 14 gauge is limited to 15-amp circuits maximum. Wire that is 12 gauge is used for 20-amp circuits and 10-gauge wire for 30-amp circuits. Higher amp circuits require heavier gauge wire.

Two 12/2 with ground wires are connected to this receptacle. One wire is bringing power into the receptacle while the other takes power away to the next receptacle in line. Black wires are always connected to the brass screws and the white wires to the silver-colored screws. Ground wires are mated together with a compression fitting with only one left long enough to be connected to the ground (green) screw on the receptacle.

Light switches are wired up differently than receptacles. The white wire coming in on the wire bringing power is directly connected to the white wire going to the light. They are connected with a wire nut. The black wire on the power-in line is connected to the switch's bottom screw and the black wire going to the light is connected to the switch's top screw. Ground wires are connected just like receptacles.

Three-way light switches, those where two separate switches operate the same lights independently, are wired up using 14/3 with ground. Again, white wires are connected together directly with a wire nut. Power goes into one three-way switch from the 14/2 with ground power supply wire and then 14/3 with ground is run directly over to the second switch, not the light. At the second switch, the power-in black and power-in red are connected to two screws on one end of the switch and the black wire to the light on the third screw.

Dimmer switches, designed to adjust the illumination of incandescent light bulbs, are wired up just like other light switches. Instead of featuring screws to which wires are connected, dimmers are outfitted with three separate wires, black, black, and green. The white wires from both the power-in and light lines are connected directly together with a wire nut. The power-in black wire is connected to the bottom black dimmer wire with a wire nut and the black wire to the light is connected to the top black dimmer wire with a wire nut. Both bare ground wires and the green dimmer ground wire are connected together with a wire nut.

Running electrical wire is accomplished by drilling holes in wall studs and plates. Getting around corners is sometimes difficult. Here, a ½-inch angle drill is used to drill a hole at an angle that will meet with a vertical hole drilled in the top plate just below. Wire will run down from the ceiling joist area and into the wall to serve a light switch.

Electrical wire is secured to studs with staples. Wire must be stapled no farther than 8 inches from all boxes and then every 4 feet along straight horizontal or vertical runs.

Once you have run wires to your electrical boxes, use a felt-tipped marker to label them. Do this with each wire just after you have fed it into its box. This way, you will not run into any confusion once it is time to make all connections. This is especially important when running wires to fan/lights, because you will want to make sure the switches that are made up will operate the appropriate light or fan motor as expected.

To make it easier for the installation of drywall, ends of wire inside boxes are stripped of their heavy plastic sheathing and neatly folded inside boxes. For those boxes including wires for separate units, like fan/lights, label them with pieces of masking tape so that when they are pulled out after drywall operations you'll know exactly which ones are supposed to go to what switches.

Recessed ceiling lights

Recessed ceiling lights are attractive and unobtrusive. They fit relatively flush with ceilings and offer lots of illumination. As a general rule, recessed lights with an opening diameter of 6 inches will disperse light in a 6-foot diameter. Plan to install one for every 36 to 40 square feet. Wall washers are recessed lights outfitted with trim rings that focus light to only one side, generally a wall adorned with photographs or paintings. They should be placed about 3 feet away from walls.

Halo Lighting recessed light housings are easy to install. Nailing tabs at the ends of support rods are outfitted with sharp points that are secured to ceiling joists with a hammer. Locate the bottom edge of these tabs flush with the bottom of ceiling joists. An inner ring inside housings is adjustable to ensure trim rings fit flush against finished ceilings.

Once recessed light housings have been secured to ceiling joists, adjust them into position by sliding them along their support rods. Lock them into a final position by bending tabs over the rods. (Shown top of following page.)

Recessed ceiling lights are most attractive when they are all set up in line with each other. To accomplish this task, simply stretch a string across the ceiling at the point where you desire

light edges to rest. Then, secure housing edges so that they just touch the string so all remain lined up with each other. (Shown top of following page.)

When installing more than one recessed ceiling light, be certain the units are designed to be wired together in a series. In addition, some regional building departments require that recessed ceiling lights be energy efficient, allowing insulation to actually surround housings without fear of causing any fire hazards. You must understand that light bulbs create heat and housings not designed for insulation coverage can cause insulation material to catch fire.

The recessed housing shown on the following page is an energy-efficient type. A solid housing features an air space inside that works to dissipate heat. The outer housing does not get hot when its bulb is illuminated. Wiring connections are simple. Power-in black wire is connected to the light housing's black wire and the black wire that runs to the next light in line. All white wires are secured together with a wire nut and all

grounds are connected together with a wire nut. Wire is secured to the housing by a tab just inside the electrical connection box and then stapled to the closest ceiling joist.

Because you will need so many different parts while making up the wiring connections for lights, switches, and boxes, you might want to use a handy tote box, like this one from the Plano Molding Company. Along with wire nuts and staples, you'll need to install metal nailing plates along all studs where wires run through holes closer than 1½ inches to stud faces. These nailing plates will prevent drywall nails or screws from penetrating through studs and into wires.

Wall mount light fixtures

Round electrical boxes that measure 3 to 4 inches in diameter are generally used for light fixtures. Most commonly, 3-inch boxes are fine for interior lighting while the 4-inch models are used for outdoor fixtures. Some 4-inch boxes are equipped with extra screw mounts to make them suitable for either 3- or 4-inch light fixture base plates.

Not all light fixtures are designed the same. You must read, comprehend, and follow all installation instructions packaged with the fixtures you purchase. This 3-foot light bar features a separate backing plate that mounts to the electrical box and also has screw holes at each end. Because end screw hole locations might not line up with wall studs, you might have to install wall anchors to support screws. As with all lights, white wires go together, black wires go together, and ground wires go together with one leg attached to the fixture.

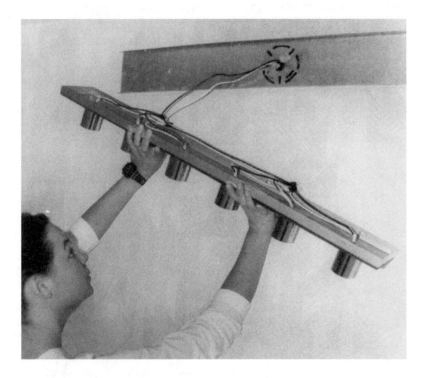

The dangers of faulty wiring are real. Each year, thousands of residential fires are started by faulty wiring and many people are injured through accidental electrocution. If you are totally unfamiliar with electrical wiring and the means by which to safely install electrical devices, hire a professional electrician to complete that phase of your bathroom remodeling work.

Overview

Shut off electrical power to all areas involved with any type of electrical alteration. Once jobs are completed and power is switched on, employ a testing device to ensure all receptacles are wired together correctly.

This handy tester from Leviton is easy to use. Simply plug it into a receptacle and note which lights illuminate at the tool's base. A chart on the tool body explains the different combinations of illuminated lights and what they mean. If problems exist in electrical circuits, information from this tester will help you to determine the necessary repairs.

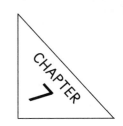

CHAPTER 7

Bathtubs, showers, & toilets

BECAUSE bathrooms are primarily designed to accommodate large volumes of water, practical persons long ago decided that there must be a means by which to control all of that water flow. Hence, we now enjoy bathtubs, shower units, and flush toilets.

Bathtubs are available in heavy cast iron or acrylic fiberglass and in lots of different colors and styles. Shower units are offered in enclosed stalls or pans that will require tile or acrylic fiberglass panels on surrounding walls. Toilets are made in lots of styles with many designed for minimal water flow. Homeowners generally select these fixtures in matching colors and styles with faucets and handles alike.

All bathtubs and showers must be served with 2-inch drainpipe that runs downhill at least ¼ inch per foot toward a main drain stack. In addition, each must be equipped with a P-trap that is generally located between floor joists or embedded in concrete floors.

Cast iron bathtubs are heavy, most weighing over 300 pounds. You will definitely need lots of help installing them. Acrylic modules weigh much less, from 60 pounds up to around 90 pounds. Regardless of the type or style selected, bathtubs must be outfitted with caulking around all their edges.

Bathtubs

Old bathtubs can be broken into pieces with a small sledge hammer to make for easiest removal. Be certain that all plumbing has been disconnected and wear safety attire, such as goggles and leather gloves. Use a utility knife to cut the caulking between the tub and tile.

Getting a new bathtub into its space will be challenging. Because most tubs measure from 14 to 22" tall (floor to top edge), they can be maneuvered into bathrooms on edge; remove the bathroom doors to accommodate access. Once a tub has been brought into the bathroom, set it upright. Place two 2-x-4 boards down on the floor in the bathtub space to serve as runners. Slide your tub on top of the 2-x-4 runners until it is in position. Then, pull out the runners and continue with the installation per the manufacturer's instructions.

Caulking around upper bathtub ledges keeps water from seeping inside walls. Along the floor, caulking prevents water from getting beneath floor vinyl and onto underlayment and subfloor materials.

Some bathtubs are designed for the addition of accessory options, like grab rails. This rail features slots at each end that slip over bolts loosely inserted into anchor mounts. Once the

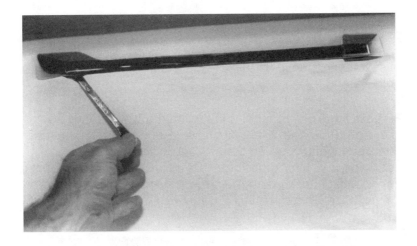

rail is in place, all you need is a wrench to tighten bolts to secure the rail.

Bathtub drain plugs operate on a simple fulcrum principle. A rod is located inside the overflow pipe and is attached to a handle. The base of the rod holds onto a heavy spring. When

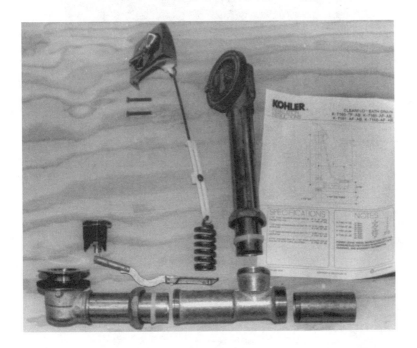

the drain plug knob is turned or flipped into the drain open position, the spring is forced down on top of the lever, which forces the drain plug to pop up. When the rod and spring are raised, the rod moves to allow the drain plug to go down and hold water.

Because bathtub drain holes are located some distance away from actual bathtub sides, pipe fittings are required to make the connections between drains, overflows, and bathroom drainpipes. With bathtubs often set inside specific cubicles, it is impossible to hook up drain and overflow pipes once bathtubs are installed. Therefore, installation instructions call for a 6- by

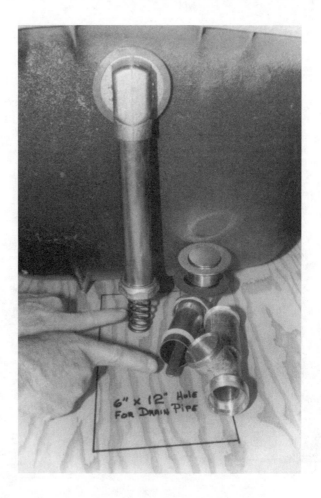

12-inch hole be placed in floors to accommodate those connections from below. With concrete floors, drainpipe must already be in position and a wall opened up to make access for this hook-up.

Overflow pipes are secured to bathtubs with a collar. A large rubber gasket fits between the overflow pipe on the bathtub side and surrounds the overflow opening. With that connection made, the drain plug rod and spring are inserted into the overflow so that the spring rests on top of the lever below.

The drain plug operating rod snaps onto the overflow housing on the inside of bathtubs. That housing is secured to the overflow head with screws. Once that task is complete, install the handle by way of a single Phillips-head screw.

Drain flanges are screwed into a pipe fitting located beneath bathtubs. To prevent these flanges from allowing water to seep past them, installers must apply a bead of plumber's putty around their perimeter. Plumber's putty is like clay. Put a wad in your hand and mold it together into a solid ball. Then place that ball of plumber's putty between your hands and work your hands back and forth turning the ball of putty into a long cylindrical rod-like shape. Lay it along the flat bottom part of the drain flange edge and gently work the ends together to

create a complete circle around the flange. Put the flange in position and screw it onto the pipe fitting below.

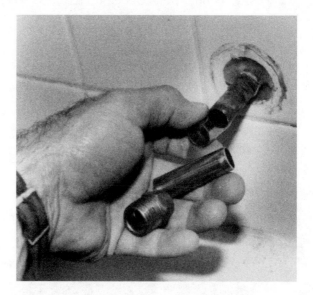

Bathtub spouts are connected to their water supply pipe by one of two methods. One entails the use of an O-ring sealed fitting and a setscrew that are slipped onto a ½-inch water supply pipe that sticks out of the finished wall by at least 2 inches. The other actually screws onto a threaded ½-inch pipe fitting that extends out from the finished wall by about 4 inches. You must read the installation instructions for the spout you are installing to learn the specific length of water supply pipe necessary. To change this existing slip-on pipe to one that will accept a threaded spout requires the installation of a ½-inch pipe collar, a short piece of ½-inch copper pipe, and a threaded male pipe fitting. All will be soldered together.

Shower units

Shower pans are placed on the floor over drains. Nailing flanges on their sides are secured to wall studs with galvanized nails, screws, or clips. Nail or screw sites along flanges must be predrilled, because trying to nail or screw through them will cause units to crack. (See top of following page.)

Shower pans are available in many different sizes. They are rigid and you must provide ample working room. The toilet must be pulled out of this bathroom to make room for the removal of the old pan and maneuvering of the new one.

Although old shower pans could be removed and new ones installed with just the first two or three rows of bottom tile removed, better looking and longer lasting results will be found when entire walls are stripped and covered with all new material. (See top of following page.)

Shower stalls are one-piece units complete with a floor and three sides. Access for their installation is critical. You must have ample room to fit units through doorways from outside your home and into the bathroom of choice. This new

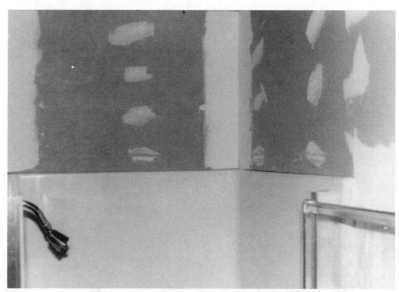

bathroom addition is outfitted with a 36- by 36-inch Kohler shower module. Two studs in an outside wall were removed to get the unit into its bathroom location. Units like this are not flexible and if they are 36 inches wide, you must provide at least 37-inch clearance through doors or other access openings. Notice that greenboard rests about ¼ inch above the unit's top rim. This was purposely done to provide room for caulking.

Shower pans are available with one or three thresholds; ledges without flanges designed for glass enclosures and doors. This 3- by 5-foot double shower pan juts into a bedroom by about 2 feet. A single shower door will be installed over just 3 feet of the threshold. To make a tight seal along the 2-foot part of the threshold that butts against a wall, 2×6s were cut to fit up and over that part of the threshold. A section of Kohler Tiling-In bead, a T-shaped material, will be placed along the threshold with one part slipped under the studs and another over stud faces onto which greenboard or backerboard will rest against. Tiling-In bead will ensure a water-tight seal along the bottom edge of the pan.

Whirlpools

Many homeowners planning for major bathroom remodeling projects opt for soothing whirlpool bathtubs in lieu of standard models. Whirlpools are equipped with a motor and pump that shoot a mixture of air and water out through jets located strategically around the tub.

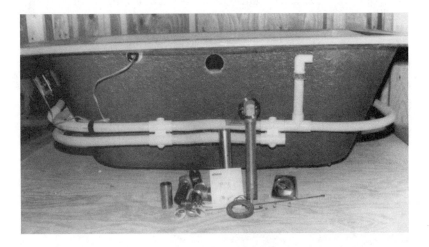

Installing bona fide hot tubs in bathrooms is not generally practical. Although some bathroom floors could be beefed up to support the tremendous weight of hot tubs constantly filled with hundreds of gallons of water, the ongoing introduction of water evaporation from hot tubs could result in significant moisture problems for the bathroom and the surrounding home interior. For a complete evaluation of the prospects for installing a hot tub in your bathroom, consult with professionals at a local hot tub dealer. They will provide you with information on ways to eliminate water evaporation and condensation problems as they relate to your specific project and home design.

This is a 5- by 3½-foot Kohler Infinity Whirlpool Bath. A wood frame will be made around it and covered with ¾-inch ACX plywood. That surface will be sealed and then covered with tile. The overflow and drain are located in the center of the unit along its 5-foot side. It is assembled and put together just like any other bathtub. A 6- by 12-inch hole provided in the floor will make access to the drain much easier from below.

Concrete floors already outfitted with a bathtub drain present a logistical problem, in that a new whirlpool's drain must also be located in the same position as the old bathtub's drain. Discuss this concern with your local whirlpool dealer before purchasing a unit.

Whirlpool baths rest on pads attached to the bottom of units. These pads are kept in place by strips of 1-x-2 wood nailed to the floor and surrounding two sides of each pad.

Whirlpools require open access through walls to motors and pumps. An extra large opening has been made at the base of this partition wall. Once drywall work has been completed, a set of doors will be installed over the opening. Afterward, a shelf unit is scheduled for installation above the doors. Whirlpool access holes are required for motor and pump servicing (shown on next page).

Motors and pumps can be located on either whirlpool unit end. You must specify which end you want them installed as it relates to the location where you can realistically install a service access hole. Likewise, particular instructions accompany all whirlpool units that explain how to secure

motors and pumps for safest and quietest operation. (Shown on the next page.)

Whirlpool motors must be supplied electrical service by a separate 120-volt 15-amp GFCI protected circuit. Nothing else

can be served by that circuit. Here, two separate 120-volt 15-amp GFCI circuits have been installed for the Infinity whirlpool; one for the motor and pump and another for the built-in water heater. Wires for both these GFCI receptacles stretch all the way and directly from the household electrical panel and separate 15-amp circuit breakers straight to the GFCIs.

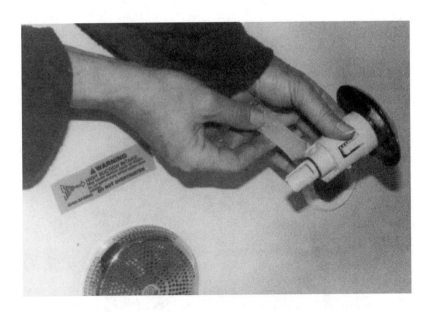

Infinity whirlpool jets are adjustable. Nozzles can be moved around inside their housings to accommodate optimum results. These jets feature an O-ring around their stem that must be lubricated before they are inserted into ports. A vial of O-ring lubricate was included with the package of optional polished-brass finished jets. An optional polished-brass cover has been installed over this whirlpool's suction inlet, replacing the standard plastic cover. Whirlpool suction units are very powerful. You must always ensure suction covers are securely in place before operating and enjoying whirlpools.

Bathtubs and whirlpools installed into roomy areas where decks will be built around them are well served with deck mount faucets and spouts; as opposed to those that attach to walls. (See top of following page.)

After deck framing has been completed, and before bathtubs or whirlpools are positioned in place, run hot and cold water supply pipes to the site where you want to install the spout and faucets. Follow installation instructions for the mounting of spouts and faucets and use caution when soldering pipe to valves. Heat from torches could damage valves; manufacturers

Bathtub & shower valves & faucets

might recommend that valves be removed from their housings during soldering operations.

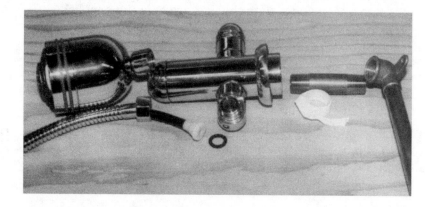

Showers are best served with a Rite-Temp Balancing Valve. From it, run a single ½-inch copper pipe up to a shower ell. This Kohler MasterShower unit screws directly onto a ½-inch copper pipe threaded nipple. A clean strap-wrench is required for its installation, because other wrenches would surely scratch the beautiful polished-brass finish.

This unit is equipped with a diverter valve that will transfer water flow to a hose and out through a body brush attachment—a most convenient option.

Toilets are served with a 3-inch drainpipe—nothing smaller. They require just one ½-inch copper pipe cold water supply. Toilets are equipped with their own P-trap, so you don't have to worry about installing one in its drain line.

After drywall has been installed, cut off the cap soldered to the supply pipe and any extra pipe that sticks out into the space. You'll only need an inch or so of pipe to make the connection with fittings supplied in the PlumbShop Toilet installation kit. (See photo above.)

Be sure to use Teflon tape on all threaded pipe parts and don't forget to slip the escutcheon onto the pipe before the fittings.

Wax rings are placed over toilet drain flanges and then toilets placed on top of closet flanges secured to the floor and glued to

the 3-inch toilet drain. Be sure that toilet anchoring bolts have been inserted into the closet flange before placing toilets in position.

Sit on the toilet to help seat the wax ring. Then use a level to ensure the unit sits plumb. Shim as necessary with metal

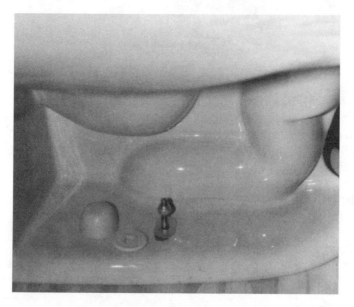

shims to secure toilets and keep them from rocking in any direction. Then, secure anchoring bolts just snugly. Do not overtighten toilet bolts, because too much torque could cause porcelain to crack. With anchor bolts snug, cover them with covers provided with your new toilet.

Toilets are generally placed on top of floor tiles or floor vinyl. During the floor finish work, toilets are removed from their floor bases and a large rag is placed inside of the drainpipe to prevent sewer gas from entering the bathroom space. Tiles and floor vinyl are then positioned up to and around the drain opening. Once the flooring material has cured, toilets are replaced using a new wax ring. Many flooring installers leave toilets in place while setting vinyl because this material is relatively easy to maneuver and cut. Tile floors present a more labor-intensive problem, however, in that each tile has to be individually nipped into a shape that will fit next to toilet base

edges. Once vinyl or tile has been cut or nipped and installed, lay down a bead of caulk between the toilet and the flooring to cover the irregular gaps and seal the area between them.

Although all toilets provide users with identical service, certain models or styles might be most appealing to you. There are plenty of shapes, designs, and colors to choose from, so take your time while shopping to select just exactly what you want. In addition, be certain to ask about low water flow models designed to save gallons and gallons of water each year. This is an especially important concern for residents in arid climates with dwindling water supplies. This Kohler San Martine Lite Toilet only requires 1.6 gallons of water per flush.

Bidets are common throughout many countries in Europe, but they are rather uncommon in normal American households. Should you want to install a bidet in your bathroom, you must be certain enough room exists for such a unit and access is available for under floor plumbing. Drain plumbing is set up just like that for toilets and a bidet's fresh water supply must include both hot and cold water lines.

Interior finish

WHETHER or not you had to install new drywall for your bathroom remodel, you will most likely have to finish walls with new paint, wallpaper, tile, wood, or other material. Whatever type of material you select for your bathroom walls, be certain to cover bathtubs, showers, and toilets with drop cloths or tarps.

Although bathtubs and showers must be installed before finishing walls, you might be better off waiting to set toilets until after wall work has been completed. This way, you will have plenty of access to wall spaces located behind toilet tanks.

One of the fastest and easiest ways to apply paint is with the Campbell Hausfeld House Painter, which is an airless painting machine equipped with a spray gun for exterior work. Use an optional paint roller attachment to minimize problems with paint drips and roller pans tipping over for interiors.

Paint & stain

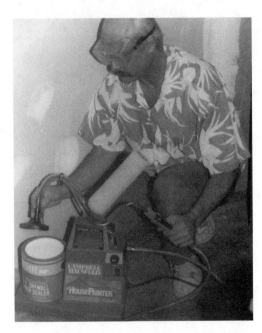

Hardwood trim around this Leslie-Locke ventilating roof window has been sealed and is now getting a coat of stain. Paint or stain work inside light wells should start from the top and work down. Once the trim has been stained and allowed to cure, place masking tape along its bottom edge to prevent drywall primer or paint from marring its surface.

Use caution while working on ladders. All Keller ladders include a label denoting the highest rung that is safe to stand on for working. Adhere to those recommendations. If you need to reach higher than one ladder will reach, opt to use a taller ladder.

Wallpaper

Wallpaper is available in prepasted or unpasted rolls. There are advantages and disadvantages to each type of application. Prepasted wallpaper must soak in a tub of water to activate paste, so you must contend with unavoidable water drops.

Unpasted wallpaper, on the other hand, will require a work table where paper is unrolled and covered on its backside with paste. A couple of sawhorses and piece of plywood work well as a temporary wallpaper workstation.

Almost any kind of wallpaper is suitable for bathrooms. However, because bathrooms are so commonly exposed to high moisture concentrations from baths and showers that could loosen wallpaper glue, you must be certain wallpaper installation is accomplished according to all manufacturers recommendations. This is especially important with regard to wall surface preparations. According to instructions, thoroughly wash the walls to remove all traces of dirt and other residue, then sand them to scuff smooth paint layers and knock down lumpy textures. Treat walls to a coat of wallcovering primer or sizing. These materials greatly assist wallpaper glue to strongly adhere to wall surfaces and remain in place—even when subjected to steamy bathroom atmospheres.

Wallpaper must be cut with a razor knife. Use caution with these tools to avoid cutting yourself and anything else near wallpaper work areas. It is very important to use sharp razor blades. Dull blades will cause paper to tear and make trimming work exceptionally difficult.

One of the best razor knives to use during wallpapering activities is the long type with break-off blade sections. This model allows users to quickly access sharp blades as soon as old tips become dull. Be careful breaking razor blade sections off and wear safety goggles during the process to avoid eye injury in case an accident occurs.

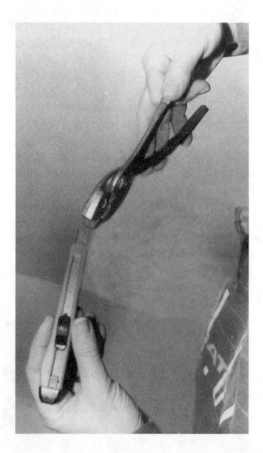

Exercise extreme caution when cutting wallpaper next to electrical wires. Turn the light switch off during wallpaper work next to the light to ensure power is cut off at that point. A slit made to the side of this wallpaper section allowed the rest of the paper to fit flat against the wall and around the light box. After the paper is trimmed straight at the ceiling, paper will be cut around the perimeter of the box away from wires. (See top of following page.)

A variety of different tile is available for all sorts of wall, countertop, and floor applications. Specific installation instructions are readily available for each different application, because they vary with the kinds of tiles used and surfaces onto which they will be applied. Sealing bathroom walls and countertops before tiling is important to prevent water from coming in contact with structural materials.

Tile

Tile is secured to walls with an adhesive like Thin-Set mortar or Mastic. Thin-Set mortar is a cement product that offers excellent adhesion and a waterproof base. Mastic is a glue-type adhesive that also has sealing and waterproofing properties. Mastic is easier to work with and not as messy as Thin-Set. Again, depending on the type of tile you install and the material onto which it will be applied to, you might not have a choice in adhesives, because installation instructions might require one over the other. (See top of following page.)

Almost every tile job will require some tiles to be cut. Always order extra tiles because some will break during the cutting process. As a general rule, purchase about 10 percent more tile than what you need. If you have some left over, save them in case one or two of the installed ones get chipped or cracked in

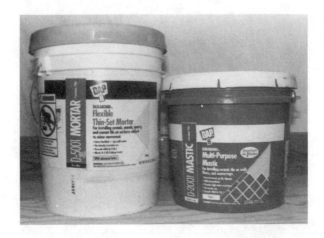

the future. This way, you'll be guaranteed that replacement tiles will match the existing ones in color, size, and texture.

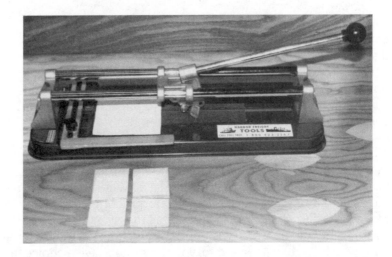

This tile cutter from Harbor Freight Tools is simple to use. The lever is attached to a round cutting head that is rolled forward along tile surfaces to cause a scoring mark. Once tile is scored, lift the lever into position and position its rear-mounted breaking pad on top of the tile. Apply downward pressure on the lever to crack tile at the scoring mark. (See top of following page.)

Tile cutters are only capable of cutting tile in a straight line. Cutting round arcs on tile to fit around plumbing pipes requires the use of tile nippers. Nippers look like a pair of pliers with flat cutting heads in lieu of serrated grips. Nip off just small chunks of tile at a time, as evidenced here with an abundance of tile chips that are a result of trimming tile to fit around a vanity's round lavatory opening.

Cutting and nipping tile requires some practice. Try your skills on old tile first to get a feel for the tools and how they work. Wear safety goggles to prevent eye injuries from flying tile debris. The nippers can really throw out slivers and chips.

Drywall repairs, mudding, and sanding have been completed on this old window opening. A thin film of Mastic is being applied to serve as a sealer; as per label instructions. This sealer film will be allowed to cure overnight to ensure that subsequent applications of Mastic with a serrated-edged trowel will not break the sealing surface. (See top of following page.)

While the Mastic seal cures on the drywall in the bathroom, tiles have been placed on the rebuilt vanity top to determine

how they could be positioned best. For this application, a center line at the middle of the lavatory opening was established and tiles set to it. The rest were placed around them.

Planning any tile job before spreading Thin-Set or Mastic is very important. Locate the center of the area you want to tile and use a level to make a perfectly straight vertical pencil line. Then, set loose tiles in position all the way to the wall on both sides. See how the pattern looks and move tiles to the right or left of the line as necessary to prevent the need for installing narrow tiles in either corner. If at all possible, plan your tile job so tiles do not have to be cut any smaller than half their width.

Regular ceramic tiles measure 4¼ inches square. Other sizes are available, as are trim pieces in a variety of sizes and shapes. The edges of this vanity top will be covered with oak trim, so there is no need to install round-edged tile trim pieces.

A straight line was made using a guide that stretched from the top of the tiles on one side to the tops of those on the other. This line will serve as a gauge for the application of tile Mastic. Only spread enough Mastic or Thin-Set that can be easily covered with tile in no more than twenty minutes. Instructions for Mastic and Thin-Set describe what size notched trowel to use for various tile applications. Larger tiles require bigger notches to provide more material for bonding. Have a clean rag handy to wipe away drips of Mastic that fall on existing tile.

Small ridges spaced on the sides of most ceramic tiles permit installers to easily place tiles a proportional distance away from each other. This allows equal room between all tiles for grout.

Sometimes, tile ridges don't mate exactly and you will have to use a straightedge to gauge their vertical or horizontal position. For tiles without ridges, you can use plastic guides shaped like an addition sign (+). These guides are made in different sizes for various tile sizes. They are placed at tile corners to keep tiles evenly spaced.

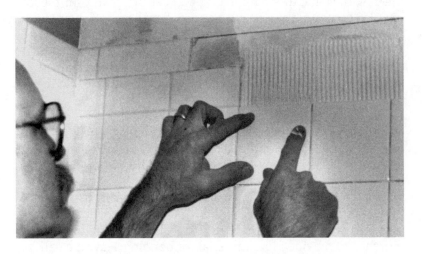

After a row or two of tiles have been set in place, wrap a board in a towel or piece of carpet. Place the board against tiles and lightly tap with a hammer. Tapping too hard might cause tiles to move or slide out of place. All you want to do with this operation is make sure each tile rests against the wall evenly.

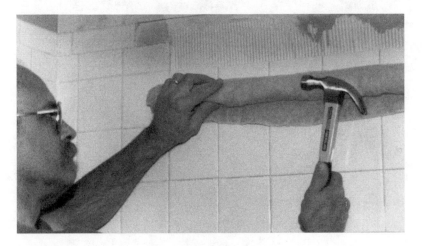

After tapping tiles, you might notice Mastic or Thin-Set has oozed into grout spaces. Use a clean putty knife to remove excess adhesive to ensure plenty of room will remain between tiles for grout.

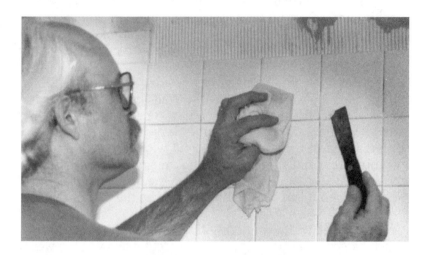

Periodically, stand back away from your tile job and check out your work. Looking at tile from a distance will enable you to detect any obviously abnormal tile positions. Adjust them as necessary before adhesive dries. Do not slide tiles around on Mastic. If need be, pull a misplaced tile off of the wall, clean it off, apply a new band of adhesive and replace the tile.

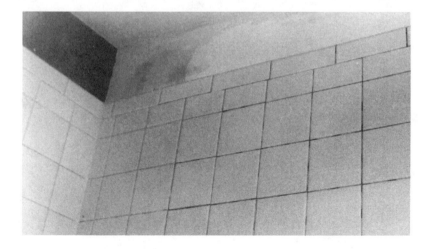

Tile must cure for at least 24 hours before grout can be applied. Drying times vary according to temperature and humidity, so be sure to read the application instructions on your grout container.

Grout is available in a variety of colors, some with sand as an additive and others without. Generally, large tiles with wide grout spaces require sanded grout for added strength. Regular 4¼- by 4¼-inch ceramic tiles call for grout with no sand.

Grout comes in containers as a dry powder. It is mixed proportionately with water. The DAP Wall Grout used for this job calls for a little over 3 parts grout to 1 part water. Label directions illustrate how much grout is required for certain square foot areas. It is best to start out with a smaller amount of grout while mixing with water than too much. This way, if too much water is initially poured into the pail with grout, additional grout can be added to thicken up the mixture.

Grout is mixed with water until it becomes thick and heavy, much like peanut butter. If you apply grout when it is too wet, it will flow out of grout spaces. If it is applied too thick, you will have a tough time forcing grout completely into the spaces between tiles. Apply tile grout with a soft rubber faced trowel. Once all spaces have been adequately filled, use a damp sponge

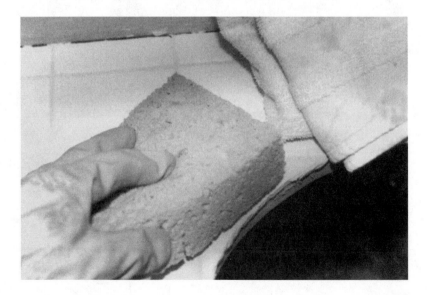

or cloth to wipe away excess grout. Be careful not to apply so much pressure on a sponge or cloth that you remove too much grout from between tile.

Once the bulk of extra grout has been wiped away, use a soft clean dry towel or cloth to remove residue. You might notice a fine film on tiles later, which is normal. Clean it off the following day with a damp cloth. Keep grout moist with a spray bottle or damp cloth for 24 hours after application.

Floors

Only certain types of tiles are suitable for floor applications. In addition, floor underlayment must conform to specific recommendations to avoid damage to tiles and grout. Your local tile dealer can explain all the differences in tiles, their advantages, disadvantages, and best methods of application.

With any tile job, you must start out with loose tiles to determine an appropriate starting point. In many cases, tile installers start out with a pencil line directly in the center of a bathroom doorway. They lay tiles out from that point to see how the ends fall. If one end results in less than a tile width past the last full tile, the entire pattern can be pushed over the other way so that those last tiles placed against the wall will be at least as wide as half the tile's width.

Wood subfloors must be covered with ½-inch ACX plywood for tile floor installations. Plywood sheets must have a gap of ⅛ inch between them on all edges. Before tile is installed, the plywood must be sealed with a specific product compatible with the tile and adhesive that will be used.

Secure vinyl floors with vinyl flooring adhesive, a material very similar in texture to Mastic. Some brands require all floor areas be covered with adhesive while others only recommend adhesive be placed along perimeter edges. Use a sharp razor knife to cut vinyl around corners and other obstacles. Install threshold strips in doorways to cover vinyl flooring open edges. Nail or glue base molding or cove molding around the base of walls. (See top of following page.)

Floor underlayment scheduled for floor vinyl must be made smooth. For this, patching material was designed to be spread over floors to fill cracks, divots, and other imperfections.

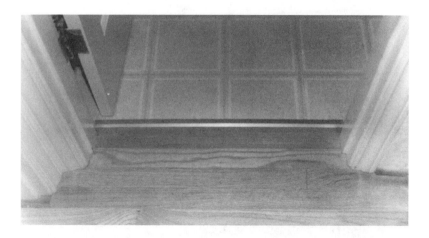

Apply patching material with a trowel, much like drywall mud.

Even though attractive shower curtains might help to beautify some bathrooms, they are not nearly as capable of keeping water inside shower enclosures as well as doors. Consider the addition of shower doors to minimize the damaging effects of water spreading out of bathtubs and onto floor and wall surfaces.

Shower doors

Single shower doors consist of wall jambs on the sides, a curb at the threshold, and door. They are installed on shower only units. Bypass shower doors are designed for bathtubs and those shower pan units with wide thresholds. Along with wall jambs and curbs, they require a header and two shower door panels.

Shower door installations for shower stall units might require lower wall jamb ends be filed to match the contour of the threshold edge. Wall jambs must rest flat against walls and thresholds. (See top of next page.)

Follow all instructions in sequence to result in quality shower door installations. Draw marks on the threshold to determine its center line, then place a wall jamb with its threshold end filed on the threshold to straddle the center line marks. Here, a level was used to assist in setting the wall jamb plumb while a felt-tipped marker was used to denote wall anchor positions. (See bottom of next page.)

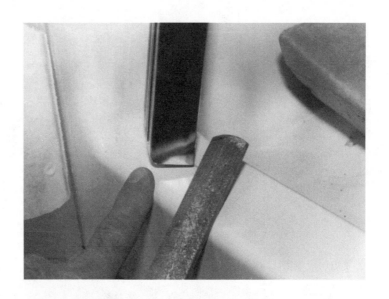

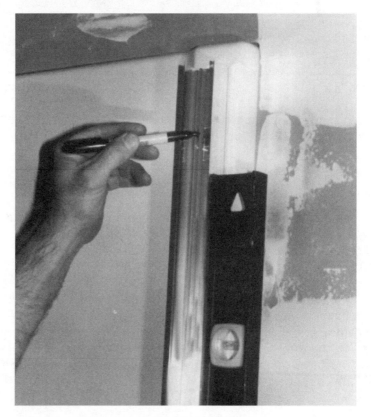

Use regular drill bits to drill through acrylic fiberglass shower enclosure jambs for the insertion of wall anchors. For tile, you must use concrete drill bits. Because tile could easily crack during any drilling operation, apply only light pressure while drilling. To help drill bits get started and prevent them from walking, lightly tap a small sharp nail against the spot you want to drill and gently make a slight chip in the surface. The wall anchors supplied with this Kohler shower door package require a ³⁄₁₆-inch hole. In tile, drill a much smaller pilot hole first. Follow it with a ³⁄₁₆-inch bit.

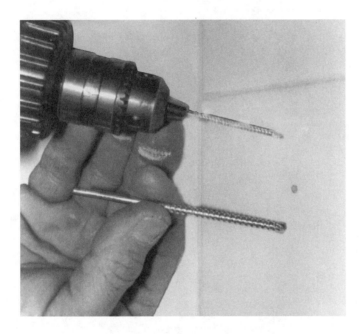

This wall anchor was simply compressed and then inserted into the ³⁄₁₆-inch hole. A few light hammer taps helped to make the anchor rest flush against the surface. (See top of following page.)

This wall jamb was secured to the tile wall with three screws driven into their anchors. The black objects located at the top and bottom of this wall jamb are adjusting blocks. Threaded inserts were screwed in or out as a means to adjust the wall jamb filler piece that goes on next. (See bottom of following page.)

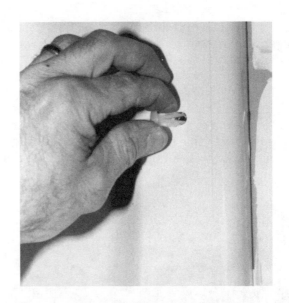

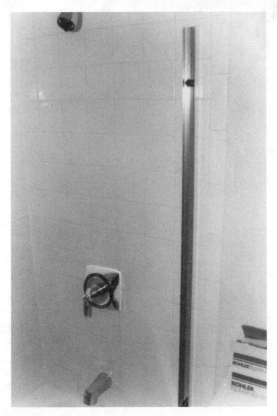

120 Bathrooms: Remodeling projects

Holes in filler jambs line up with adjusting blocks so that a Phillips-head screwdriver can fit through them to operate the block inserts. Use a level to help set filler jambs vertically plumb. Move adjusting blocks in or out to help stabilize and hold filler jambs in their plumb position.

For this bypass shower door system, a molded plastic bypass seal was compressed and fitted into a groove featured along the filler jamb. The outer shower door panel rests against this one to prevent water from escaping outside the enclosure. On the other side, the inner shower door panel rests against the inner side of that filler jamb's bypass seal. (See top of following page.)

The chrome header across the top of these bypass shower doors was attached to wall jambs with screws. The outside door was positioned first, and the inside door second from inside the

bathtub. The only work left to do is caulk the inside edges along the curb and wall jamb. (See top of next page.)

This Kohler Pipeline Pivot shower door does not require a header. Instead, the door panel simply rests on this lower pin and is then supported at the top with a similar pin and bushing combination. Installation instructions clearly outline all caulking requirements. (See bottom of next page.)

Both bypass and pivot shower doors are adjustable to assist installers in making perfect installations every time.

Vanities

SMALL BATHROOMS AND POWDER ROOMS might not provide
sufficient room for vanity installations. For them, a pedestal
lavatory might work out better. For other bathrooms offering
more open space, the addition of a vanity could prove most
worthwhile. In addition to large doors in the front for the
storage of large items and cleaning supplies, drawers could be
installed for the storage of personal care products and other
small things.

Vanities are most commonly put together with plywood and
¾-inch-thick wood for front rails and stiles. Particleboard is not
recommended because moisture will cause it to fail and fall
apart.

Construction & installation

This is the start of a 69-inch-long, 24-inch-deep, and 32-inch-
high double lavatory vanity. It is resting on its backside while
screws are driven into the two center dividers. The unit is
assembled with ¾-inch ACX plywood with the A-sides facing in
toward two open door areas and the C-sides facing out the ends
and in toward a center drawer section. Wood glue and 1⅝-inch
drywall screws are employed to hold it all together. Both end
pieces were routed with a ¾-inch straight bit ⅜ inch deep to
allow partial insertion of the ¾-inch floor ends.

The dimensions and locations for the doors and drawers were calculated on paper before this custom vanity project began. Doors and door fronts will be ordered from Quality Doors, saving lots of work in their construction. Glue was first applied to the divider and the oak rail put into position against it and then secured with the finish nailer. A wide board was installed along the back. Screws will be driven through it and into wall studs to secure the vanity in place.

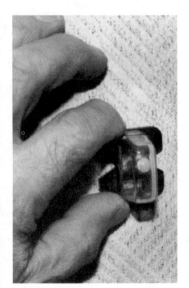

It is important to secure vanities to wall studs instead of just wall anchors inserted into drywall. Use a stud finder to help locate studs. These handy devices simply feature a magnet mounted on a swivel. When the magnet is positioned over a drywall screw or nail, it will move to a horizontal position. Finding drywall screws or nails is an easy method of locating wall studs.

Use shims under vanity edges to adjust them to a level position. Be sure vanities rest level in both their width and depth directions.

With wall stud locations noted and vanities level, use drywall or wood screws to secure units in place. All vanities must be outfitted with a board along their upper-back edge into which screws are driven and passed through into wall studs. A drill/driver makes this work progress much faster and efficiently than working with a hand-operated screwdriver.

Vanity tops

Vanity countertops are finished in plastic laminate, tile, properly sealed wood (not plywood), or any of a number of other custom countertop products.

Attach plastic laminate to countertops with contact cement. Cut laminate with a saw to a size a bit bigger than the countertop; generally allow about ¼ inch to ½ inch to overlap countertop edges. Then apply contact cement to both the countertops and backsides of laminate. Allow it to cure for a specified time, as indicated on the label; generally 15 to 30 minutes.

Place thin strips of wood on the countertop and position laminate on top of them. Once the laminate has been perfectly positioned, carefully remove the thin wood strips. Thin wood strips are employed because contact cement will bond almost instantly; there is no room for error once contact cement-coated laminate makes contact with the contact cement on the countertop. After the laminate has been securely attached to the countertop with use of a roller, use a trimmer with a laminate-cutting bit to trim the excess from the countertop edges. In corners where the trimmer cannot reach, use a sharp file.

Vanity countertops that are scheduled for tile must be sealed first. Here, scrap wood was temporarily nailed along the countertop edges to serve as a guide for tile placement. Once the tiling job is complete, I will replace the scrap wood with strips of ¾-inch-thick oak.

After the film of sealer had cured, I installed tiles using Mastic. Notice how many tiles had to be nipped to fit around the lavatory opening.

Then I placed a strip of masking tape along the bottom edge of the backsplash during grout application. I filled the area between the back row of tiles and the backsplash with caulking.

I sealed the solid-oak backsplash, treated it with stain, and then coated it with polyurethane before setting tile. This ensures that the full front face of the backsplash is sealed and stained, especially the lowest part that will be covered with tile.

Vanity drawers

Drawers are not much more than boxes outfitted with guides to allow them to slip into and out of vanities with ease. Of greatest importance is to build drawers within the tolerances suggested by drawer guide manufacturers.

Installation instructions that accompany Häfele drawer guides are specific. Depending on the style of drawer guide selected, you must make drawers about ½ inch narrower than the rail and stile openings on vanity faces. This is to allow sufficient operating room for the guides so that drawers are not difficult to operate. Drawers are generally constructed with ½-inch ACX plywood and a ¼-inch hardboard or ³⁄₁₆-inch plywood bottom. (See top of following page.)

Various drawer guide styles are designed for installation along the tops, bottoms, or sides of drawers. This system that goes

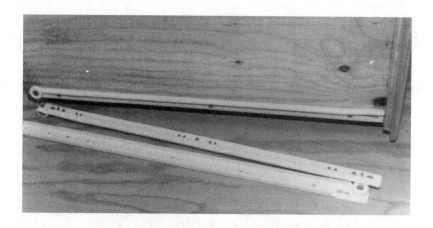

along drawer bottoms is easy to install. For vanities where stiles stick out past interior dividers or end panels creating an open space between drawer guide members and their vanity mates, you must install strips of wood behind the vanity guides for them to reach the drawers.

Working drawer front panels are cut to the same size as rear panels. For the most part, drawers are then adorned with better quality drawer face fronts. These fronts are attached to working front panels with screws driven from inside drawers.

Installing drawer handles and pulls is easy with the Häfele
Qwik-Set drill jig. Simply find the drawer front centers both
vertically and horizontally, position the jig so it is centered on
the drawer front, and then adjust the drilling hole guides to the
width of handles. Drill holes and insert handle screws in from
the backside and into handles.

Vanity refacing

Quality Doors makes it easy to make older vanities in
structurally sound condition look new. Along with custom-
made doors and drawer fronts, they offer veneers, end panels,
and hardware. You can save a lot of money by refacing your old
vanity yourself and give it a brand new appearance.

Actual wood veneer is supplied on a roll that measures 2 feet
wide by 8 feet long. It is equipped with an adhesive backing. It
cuts easily with scissors. Pencil lines made on this sheet indicate
where to cut sections destined for a number of vanity rails all the
same length. Other types of refacing material is available along
with actual wood veneer. (See top of following page.)

Simply peel off veneer backing paper and place it in its
appropriate position. According to instructions, cut veneer
½ inch wider than necessary to account for out-of-square
vanities. That excess is easily trimmed with a sharp razor knife.

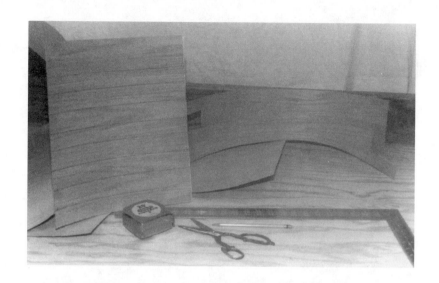

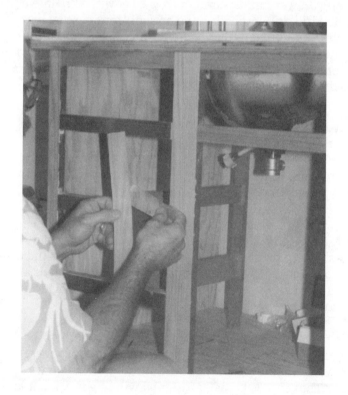

An instructional videotape available through Quality Doors
fully explains how to make back cuts when rail and stile
sections meet together at an intersection. A bit of excess
material from both pieces is overlapped. Use a wide putty knife
as a straightedge while cutting with a sharp razor knife through
both pieces. After the cut, remove all excess from both pieces to
result in a perfect joint.

Doors are attached to stiles with hinges. A variety of hinge
styles are available at home-improvement centers and through
Quality Doors. These hinges are heavy duty and fit into holes
bored into the door at the factory.

Should you prefer to paint your newly constructed vanity, be
certain to coat bare wood with a primer before applying paint.
Regular ACX plywood does not always take paint well. In lieu of
ACX plywood for vanity end panels, opt for a hardwood material,
like birch or oak. Hardwood plywood accepts paint and stain very
well to offer fine-looking results. (See top of following page.)

The end panel on this rebuilt vanity will be covered with a piece
of ³⁄₁₆-inch hardwood plywood glued to it. Notice how the paint

job appears a bit rough. Had this existing end panel been constructed with hardwood plywood, the paint job would look excellent. All of the new wood veneer, doors, drawer fronts, and end panel will be sealed, stained, and then coated with polyurethane to match the vanity's backsplash.

Sinks & faucets

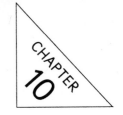

VANITY LAVATORY and faucet selections are vast. Along with sizes and styles, you can choose from many different colors and finishes. Before starting out on your lavatory and faucet shopping spree, measure the existing vanity countertop to ensure a comparably sized top will accommodate your lavatory and faucet selection.

Pedestal lavatories require no vanity because they rest on their own pedestal.

Drainpipes are hidden from view inside the pedestal and only the water supply valves and some hose are visible. Pedestal lavatories are secured to walls with screws as well as supported by their pedestal.

Lavatory installation

New Kohler lavatories are packaged with templates. These templates are cut out and then traced with a pencil onto new vanity tops. Tops slated for plastic laminate should have the laminate installed first before cutting openings for lavatories. This way, the opening will be perfect and you will not have to hassle with cutting laminate to fit an existing hole.

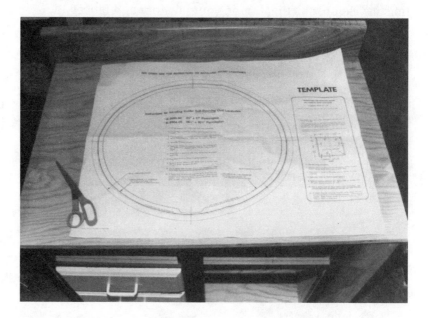

Find the center point of your vanity top along its width. Determine where you want the lavatory to set with regard to depth. Use template guidelines to help position it squarely on the top. Do not place the lavatory too close to the front vanity face where the upper-front rail is located. Lavatory openings cut too close to the fronts of units could result in rails obstructing the front part of the opening. Use masking tape to hold templates in place while tracing around them. (See top of following page.)

Once the lavatory outline has been made on the new top, use a drill to make a hole along the inside edge of the tracing. This hole must be big enough for a jigsaw blade to fit into. Carefully operate the jigsaw around the pencil line to cut out the lavatory opening. (See bottom of following page.)

Jigsaw blades might not be able to make intricate curves in one pass as outlined on the template. For those curves, use a series of back cuts to slowly accomplish the cutting task. This projection is needed for the overflow passage molded into the lavatory. Notice the hole that was drilled on the opening's waste side just above the head of the jigsaw for its blade. (See top of following page.)

Faucets Lavatory styles that do not incorporate separate openings for faucets offer a means by which to locate faucets anywhere along the vanity top desired. Normally, deck-mount faucets are positioned in the center of lavatories; except those designed for narrow vanities, like the Boutique model.

The outer portion of this template includes instructions and guidelines on how to determine the center of the lavatory for the drilling of access holes for the faucet. Because this double vanity is designed with doors on each end and a set of drawers in the middle, lavatories were centered in the middle of door openings. Notice the use of a tape measure and a pencil line made on the vanity top. (See top of following page.)

A 1-inch hole will be drilled in the top at the center of the sink opening to make access for the faucet spout. Although the stem for the spout is much smaller than 1 inch, extra room is required for the drain plug operating rod that fits behind the spout. (See bottom of following page.)

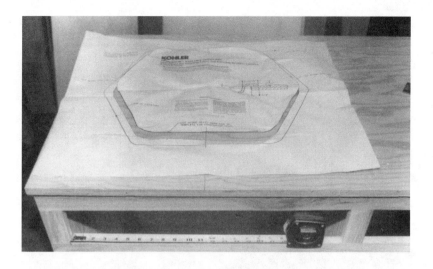

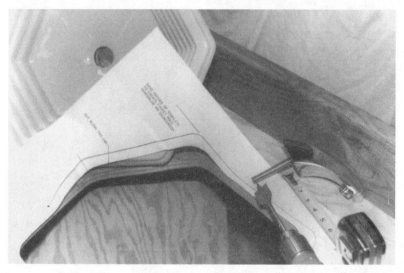

This Kohler Coralais faucet system features individual water valves and handles that can be located anywhere around the lavatory. Once their position is determined, holes must be drilled in the top for their installation. All holes will be drilled before the application of tile to this vanity top. Tiles will then be cut and nipped as needed to fit around holes. (See following page.)

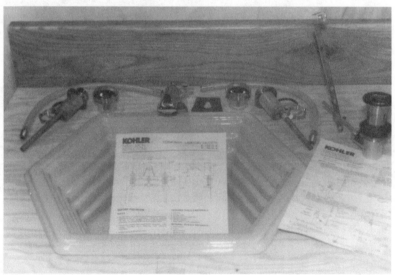

Faucets with individual valves and spouts are put together a bit differently than one-piece units. Water is supplied to the valves normally by way of supply hoses run from valves at the wall. Then, another set of hoses are run from the separate hot and cold water valves and into a T screwed onto the spout stem. Here, a compression fitting must be installed on the end of the valve supply tube to make up the connection to the water supply hose.

Compression fittings consist of a special female threaded nut (threads on the inside) and ferrule, which attaches to the male threads (threads on the outside) of a valve or other pipe. The compression fitting nut has a hole in the middle of it that allows it to be slipped over a water supply pipe. To install such a fitting, slip the nut over the supply pipe with its threads pointing out so that they can be engaged with the threads on the valve. Next, slip on the ferrule. Position the valve's male threads next to the pipe and move the compression nut over the ferrule and begin screwing it onto the valve. As the nut is tightened, the ferrule will be compressed between it and the valve to create a watertight compression fitting connection.

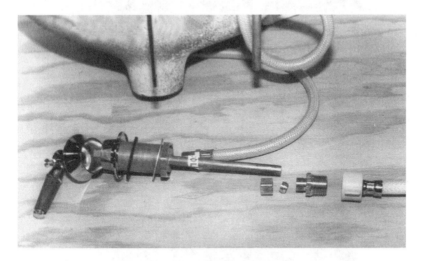

Secure faucets to vanity tops with large washers and nuts that fit over stems. Then screw water supply hoses onto those stems with hot water on the left and cold on the right. Be sure to wrap Teflon tape onto pipe threads before attaching and tightening supply line hook-ups. Teflon tape is wrapped onto threads in a clockwise direction, the same direction that you will turn connectors to put them on.

Lavatories are secured to vanity tops in different manners. Some require clips and others just need to rest on top of sealant. The lavatory for this vanity opening was put in place and a pencil line traced around its outer perimeter. The lavatory was removed and then two beads of sealant spread around the opening—one close to the opening edge and the other close to the pencil line. I will use a putty knife to quickly spread sealant over the entire area were the lavatory rim will rest.

Once lavatories are inserted into their openings and secured, work can begin on the plumbing. New lavatories placed on existing vanities might require that their drainpipes be cut to fit correctly. Lavatory drains will empty into the front side of the P-trap and then a pipe from the P-trap will attach to the drain stub that sticks out of the wall. Drain line connectors only need to be tightened hand tight, while all water supply lines must be torqued with a wrench.

Lavatory drain flanges must be outfitted with a ring of plumber's putty before being screwed onto their tail piece located underneath. Wipe away excess putty that has squeezed out after the connection with a clean paper towel.

After installing all plumbing drains and water lines under vanities, take a moment to go over your work to make sure you have completed all tasks as recommended by installation instructions. After you are convinced your job was done correctly, turn on the water and inspect for leaks. Tighten connections as necessary to stop leaks.

CHAPTER 11

Amenities

WHILE PLANNING for your bathroom remodeling endeavors, do not overlook potentials for extra amenities. Creature comforts small and large can go a long way toward making your bathroom much more convenient, efficient, and comfortable.

Amenity ideas are abundant in homeowner and do-it-yourself magazines, plumbing fixture dealer showrooms, and home-improvement centers. Once your bathroom remodeling budget has been established, shop around to see what types of amenities might fit within it. After all, you are expecting to complete most or all of the work yourself, so look at the money you'll save as a means to afford a few extras.

Roof windows

Roof windows are made of glass and skylights from acrylic. Leslie-Locke offers quite a few different styles and sizes of roof windows and skylights, including those that open up to fresh air. Units are available that feature Low-E double-pane glass with an argon fill between them for highest energy efficiency. Installation instructions are clear and units are easy to install.

Light wells under roof windows must be framed with 2-x-4 lumber, covered with drywall, and insulated on the attic side. Light wells can be constructed to run directly down from roof windows or splayed out to encompass a longer area past roof window ends. Here, a simple 2-x-4 box frame has been installed at the end of a roof window light well. Drywall will be screwed to it. (See top of following page.)

On roof window light well sides, space 2×4s 16 to 24 inches apart. They are needed to support drywall. An easy way to accomplish this task is by holding boards up to the opening and marking across their face with a pencil at both rafter and ceiling joist intersections. (See bottom of following page.)

The Makita Slide Compound saw makes quick work of cutting 2×4s at prescribed angles.

At the shallow end of this roof window light well, a piece of
½-inch drywall is used as a gauge to determine the correct
position for the box frame that needs to be fitted between the
roof truss members. Ideally, roof windows should be centered
inside roof openings so that drywall can easily slip in behind
trim to conceal its rough edges and make for a clean
installation.

You can cut drywall at the same angle as splayed light well
frames by using a bevel tool. This instrument features a wood
handle with a movable metal neck. Simply loosen the locking
wing nut and position the handle flat with the bottom of the
light well frame and maneuver the metal neck against the
upright frame member. Twist the wing nut to lock the metal
arm in position. (See top of following page.)

With the bevel tool locked at the identical angle of the splayed
light well, place its handle squarely against the edge of drywall
and make a pencil line down the metal arm. Increase the
length of that pencil line with use of a long straightedge. Write

down the measurements along the perimeter of the splayed light well to use as a reference.

With help from the bevel, mark the measurements on the drywall panel and draw lines to intersect all corners. Then check the measurements again to ensure the piece will fit properly before it is cut. Because all drywall corners and exposed edges will be covered with drywall mud, paper, or metal bead, cut drywall just a shade smaller than the opening calls for. This will make it much easier for you to actually place drywall panels into position.

Because all roof rafters and trusses are not always set to precisely 16 or 24 inches on center, you might find that drywall does not fit snugly between light well framing and roof window trim. In those cases, use wood shims to push top drywall edges out from roof framing members and up tight against roof window trim.

Roof window and skylight light wells must be insulated with the same material used for attics. Insulation can be installed before drywall just like regular walls and ceilings. Or, you could install it after the light well has been covered with drywall. Either way, you must cut pieces to fit and allow room at the ceiling level for its insulation batts.

Bathrooms that do not have windows are required to have a fan. Fans are useful in all bathrooms because not everyone remembers to open windows during or immediately after showering. Remember, moisture is a major bathroom problem that can cause paint to peel, wallpaper to come loose, and a host of other problems in a relatively short time. Ideally, bathrooms should be equipped with fans that turn on each time lights are illuminated, especially for children.

A lot of fans are located directly above a bathtub/shower, which is great for removing moist bathroom air and forcing it outdoors.

The NuTone Bathroom Exhaust Fan/Light Combination features a regular 100-watt incandescent light socket and a smaller one for a 25-watt night light. Three separate switches are required to operate those features. (See top of following page.)

With the light unit and fan removed, install the unit housing above a new shower enclosure. Housing rods are adjustable and the housing can be moved along the rods until positioned as desired. Secure rods to ceiling joists with screws. (See bottom of following page.)

Bathroom fans

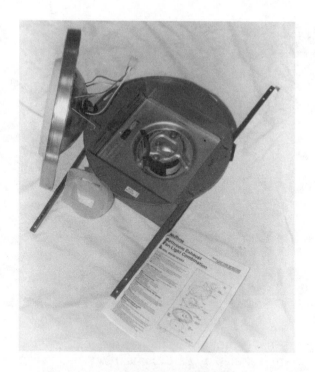

150   Bathrooms: Remodeling projects

Feed electrical wire through an opening that has been outfitted with an electrical clamp. Once enough wire has been fed into the box with about 6 inches extra extending out to work with, cinch screws down on the clamp to compress a small bar against the wire to keep it in place and secure.

Three separate wires must be run from the switch box to this fan/light unit. Be sure to label wires at each end so you will know which ones to hook up to which wires and switches. Installation instructions clearly point out which colored unit wires supply power to each light and the fan.

Exhaust ducting must be secured to the fan housing and then run to an exhaust vent attached to an exterior wall. Many building departments now require exhaust ducting be made of metal. In lieu of plastic ducting, flexible aluminum ducting is available at home-improvement centers.

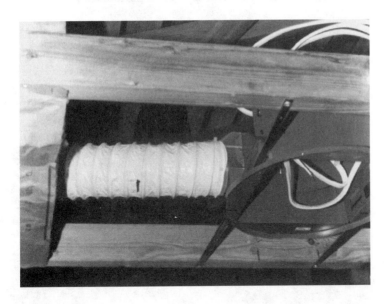

Fan housings should remain empty until all drywall work has been completed. Afterward, replace the fan motor and secure it in place with its Phillips-head screw. Then, plug in the fan and light units into their respective sockets. The light unit is secured to the bottom of the fan frame with a special screw. Install light bulbs and replace the outer lens cover.

The switches for fan/lights are wired up just like any other light switch. All white wires are connected together with a large red wire nut. Ground wires secured together with one leg attached to the light switch grounding screw. Individual black wires are then connected to their appropriate switch.

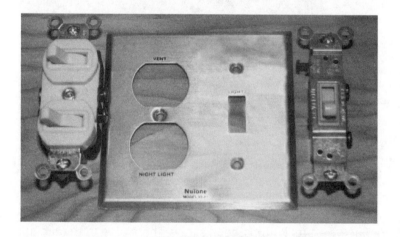

Power to the light switches will come from a single power-in wire. Its white and ground wires will be connected to the others for the lights and fan. To get power to the three individual light and fan switches, three short pieces of black wire will be connected to the power-in black wire with a large red wire nut. One black wire will then be connected to each separate switch.

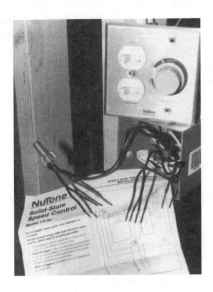

Baseboard and wall-mounted electric bathroom heaters can be moved as long as they are positioned away from water sources (i.e., tubs, showers, and lavatories). Most often, heaters are located opposite lavatories and are about 3' away from tubs or showers. Electric heaters are held in position with screws that fasten their housings to wall studs. Electric wires protrude through walls and into heater units. Moving heaters will require electrical supply wires be routed to a new heater location.

Bathroom heater

Before working with any wires, be certain that power has been shut off to them at the main electrical circuit breaker panel. Access to electrical wires can be made under wood floors, in the crawl space or basement, or in the attic space—it all depends on how the existing heater wires are run. For bathrooms located on top of concrete slab floors or on second story levels where the route of existing wires is not through the attic, you will have to cut away drywall and open up walls to facilitate routing new wires through wall studs.

Note: If you have to add a section of electrical wire to the end of an existing heater wire, you must install an electrical box, like those for receptacles and switches, at the point where the new and old wires are connected. Fasten the appropriate wires together with wire nuts, place them inside the box, and then cover the box with a solid plate. Wire connections cannot be made and then simply pushed into a wall; they must be confined inside a box and protected with a solid cover plate.

Home bathrooms located in remote corners a long way from heaters can be chilly on cold winter mornings. For those bathrooms, consider a separate wall mounted heater.

This NuTone model can be operated by a 120-volt or 240-volt power supply. A simple wiring maneuver is all it takes to make it operate on one or the other. Wall heaters must be located away from bathtubs and showers and never behind towel bars or racks. Close to water, they might pose an electrical shock hazard, and too close to combustibles is a major fire hazard.

This wall heater's frame is outfitted with holes through which screws are driven into a wall stud for support. For 240-volt operation, it should be connected to a 15-amp branch circuit. Wired for 120-volt operation, use 12/2 with ground wire and hook up to a 20-amp circuit. Be sure to follow all installation instructions, especially with regard to actual placement and wiring requirements (see top of following page).

Door handles

New door handles or knobs might be the finishing touch that makes your new bathroom remodel complete. They are easy to install, especially if all you have to do is replace old ones with new.

Weiser Lock offers a host of different door knobs, handles, and locks in a variety of shapes and designs. Because this bathroom has been remodeled with chrome faucets and accents, the handle on the bathroom side is chrome. On the hallway side, the handle is brass to match the home decor in that area.

This privacy handle set features a lock on the bathroom handle. It can be unlocked from the outside by inserting a thin

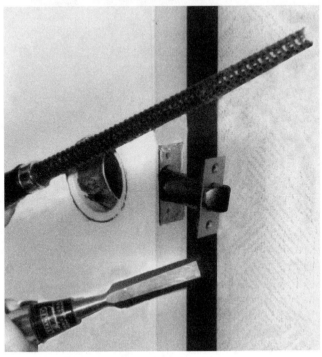

pointed object in through an access hole in the handle. Bathroom privacy locks should be outfitted with a means to unlock them from the outside in case small children lock themselves in the bathroom by mistake or someone is injured and cannot unlock the door.

The old inexpensive door handle that was removed from this door featured a latching mechanism that was smaller than the one with the Weiser Lock set. Therefore, a round rasp was employed to enlarge the hole. A sharp chisel was then used to cut out thin strips of wood at the latch plate so it would snugly fit into the recess.

Latch plates are covered with a thin film to protect them against scratching. Remember to remove this film after all installation work has been completed.

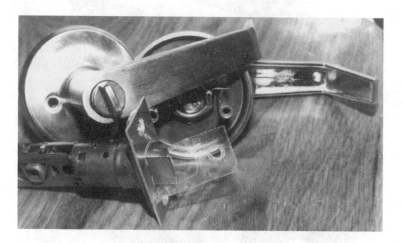

Medicine cabinets & shelf units

Medicine cabinet designs have improved tremendously over the years. Beautiful units are widely available at home-improvement centers at economical costs. Various models are designed for installation into wall framed recesses, while others simply mount directly to wall surfaces.

In this bathroom wall, 2×4s were secured horizontally between two wall studs. They are located at the top and bottom of a recessed medicine cabinet. Holes on the inside walls of the cabinet are provided for screws that secure it to side studs. You must read the instructions for the cabinet you install to determine the appropriate framing dimensions for it. Electrical boxes on both center sides of the cabinet note the locations of two lights mounted on each side of the medicine cabinet.

Direct wall mount medicine cabinets must be secured to wall studs with screws. Locate studs with a stud finder. Determine the height at which you want the medicine cabinet to rest and then measure the distance from the top of the vanity below to the bottom of the cabinet. Use boards and paint cans to build a small platform for the cabinet to rest on as a means to help you keep it in position during installation. You should also enlist the support of a helper. (See top of next page.)

Certain that the medicine cabinet sits at the correct height and centered over the vanity, drill a pilot through the horizontal support board directly in front of the wall stud. Then drive in a long wood or drywall screw. The screw should penetrate the stud by at least 1 inch. Place a level on top of the cabinet, adjust the unit plumb, and then repeat the screw installation process for the second wall stud.

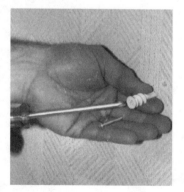

Medicine cabinets with heavy mirrors must be secured directly to wall studs. Light-weight shelf units that will not be expected to hold any great weight can be secured to walls with stout wall anchors and screws. The type shown here is simply screwed into drywall with a Phillips-head screwdriver and without need for a pilot hole.

The mounting boards located along the top and bottom of this small shelf unit only span over one wall stud on the right side. The left side was secured with wall anchors. (See following page.)

This bathroom has certainly undergone a complete face-lift. A little more finish work is needed, like putting the edge trim on

the vanity and staining the new shelf to match the vanity backsplash. A couple of pictures and a plant or two will make nice additions.

A wide variety of towel bars are available at home-improvement centers. Some models feature brackets that are secured to wall studs with screws or drywall with anchors, onto which towel bar arms are slipped over and then held secure by a setscrew located at the bottom of the arm. Arms on other models are simply screwed to walls. Because most towel bar arms will not be located directly over studs, use heavy-duty drywall anchors or Molly bolts. Packages of drywall anchors and Molly bolts will specify which size hole to drill in drywall for their installation. When drilling through tile, be sure to use a concrete drill bit; as demonstrated during the shower door installation. Towel bars can be located anywhere desired and are generally around 36" to 40" off of the floor.

Toilet paper holders are secured to vanity end panels with short wood screws. Use drywall anchors or Molly bolts when installing them on walls. Recessed toilet paper holders are secured to vanity end panels with a bracket that is tightened from inside vanities. Recessed wall openings must provide a wood frame to which holders are secured with screws on both sides.

I hope this book has helped you accomplish what you set out to do, that all your bathroom remodeling efforts flow smoothly and result in pleasing you to your absolute delight.

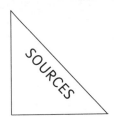

THE FOLLOWING COMPANIES and organizations were asked to participate in this book project because of the excellent quality of their products, installation and operating instructions, technical assistance, and customer service. You are highly encouraged to contact them for additional information, brochures, and product catalogs.

Alta Industries
P.O. Box 2764
Santa Rosa, CA 95405
(707) 544-5009
Tool belts, pouches, and related products

American Plywood Association
P.O. Box 11700
Tacoma, WA 98411
(206) 565-6600
Loads of information and building plans for plywood

American Tool Companies, Inc.
P.O. Box 337
DeWitt, NE 68341
(402) 683-2315
Vise-Grips; Quick-Grips; and assorted tools

Autodesk Retail Products
11911 North Creek Parkway South
Bothell, WA 98011
(800) 228-3601
Home plans computer software

Behr Process Corporation
3400 West Segerstrom Avenue
Santa Ana, CA 92704
(800) 854-0133
Paint, stain, varnish, sealers, and more

Campbell Hausfeld
100 Production Drive
Harrison, OH 45030
(513) 367-4811
Air compressors, pneumatic tools, and accessories

Cedar Shake and Shingle Bureau
515-116th Avenue NE, Suite 275
Bellevue, WA 98004-5294
(206) 453-1323
Information regarding cedar shakes and shingles

DAP, Inc.
P.O. Box 277
Dayton, OH 45401
(800) 568-4554
Glue, sealer, caulk, and assorted products

Eagle Windows and Doors
375 East Ninth Street
Dubuque, IA 52004
(319) 556-2270
Energy efficient wood windows and doors

Empire Brushes, Inc.
U.S. 13 North
P.O. Box 1606
Greenville, NC 27835-1606
(919) 758-4111
Brushes, brooms, and numerous accessories

Freud
P.O. Box 7187
High Point, NC 27264
(800) 472-7307
Biscuit cutter and other tools

General Cable Company (Romex®)
4 Tesseneer Drive
Highland Heights, KY 41076
(606) 572-8000
Fax: (606) 572-9634
Electrical wire of all kinds

Häfele America Company
3901 Cheyenne Drive
P.O. Box 4000
Archdale, NC 27263
(910) 889-2322
Cabinet and furniture hardware of all kinds

Halo Lighting, Brand of Cooper Lighting
400 Busse Road
Elk Grove Village, IL 60007
(708) 956-8400
Recessed ceiling lights

Harbor Freight Tools (a division of Central Purchasing, Inc.)
3491 Mission Oaks Boulevard
Camarillo, CA 95008
(800) 423-2567
Huge selection of home-improvement tools, supplies, and more

Keller Industries, Inc.
18000 State Road Nine
Miami, FL 33162
(800) 222-2600
Wide variety of ladders, attic stairways, and accessories

Kohler Company
444 Highland Drive
Kohler, WI 53044
(414) 457-4441
High-quality bathroom fixtures and accessories

Leslie-Locke, Inc.
4501 Circle 75 Parkway, Suite F-6300
Atlanta, GA 30339
Roof windows, skylights, ducting, ornamental iron, and more

Leviton Manufacturing Company, Inc.
59-25 Little Neck Parkway
Little Neck, NY 11362-2591
(718) 229-4040
Electrical outlets, switches, and related products

Makita U.S.A., Inc.
14930 Northam Street
La Mirada, CA 90638-5753
(714) 522-8088
Power tools and equipment of all kinds

McGuire-Nicholas Company, Inc.
2331 Tubeway Avenue
City of Commerce, CA 90040
(213) 722-6961
Tool belts, pouches, knee pads, back braces, and a lot more

NuTone
Madison and Red Bank Roads
Cincinnati, OH 45227-1599
(513) 527-5100
Built-in convenience products of all kinds

Owens-Corning Fiberglas Insulation
Fiberglas Tower
Toledo, OH 43659
(800) 342-3745
Pink building insulation of all kinds

PanelLift Telpro, Inc.
Route 1, Box 138
Grand Forks, ND 58201
(800) 441-0551
Drywall lift equipment

Plano Molding Company
431 East South Street
Plano, IL 60545-1601
(800) 874-6905
Plastic tool boxes, storage units, and shelves of all kinds

PlumbShop (a division of Brass-Craft)
39600 Orchard Hill Place
Novi, MI 48376
(810) 305-6000
Plumbing supplies for all occasions

Power Products Company-SIMKAR
Cayuga and Ramona Streets
Philadelphia, PA 19120
(215) 831-7766
Fluorescent lighting products of all kinds

Quality Doors
603 Big Stone Gap Road
Duncanville, TX 75137
(800) 950-3667
Cabinet doors, drawer fronts, and refacing materials

Simpson Strong-Tie Connector Company, Inc.
1450 Doolittle Drive
San Leandro, CA 94577
(800) 999-5099
Metal connectors for all types of construction

The Stanley Works
1000 Stanley Drive
New Britain, CT 06053
(800) 551-5936
Tools, hardware, closet organizers, and more

Sta-Put Color Pegs, Inc.
23504-29th Avenue West
Lynnwood, WA 98036-8318
Plastic pegboard hooks that stay in place

Structron Corporation
1980 Diamond Street
San Marcos, CA 92069
(619) 744-6371
Garden and construction tools; shovels, rakes, etc.

Tyvek Housewrap (DuPont)
Chestnut Run WR-2058
Wilmington, DE 19880-0722
(800) 448-9835
High-quality Housewrap

U.S. Ceramic Tile Company
P.O. Box 338
East Sparta, OH 44626
(216) 866-5531
Ceramic tile of all kinds

Weiser Lock
6660 South Broadmoor Road
Tucson, AZ 85746
(602) 741-6200
High-quality door knobs, handles, and locks

Western Wood Products Association
522 SW Fifth Avenue
Portland, OR 97204-2122
(503) 224-3930
Information about western wood products

Zircon Corporation
1580 Dell Avenue
Campbell, CA 95008
(408) 866-8600
Water levels and other devices

Illustrations are in **boldface**.